Heartbreak Hotel

Praise for Jeremy Reed

'Brilliant and special' Marc Almond

'Who better than Jeremy Reed to cast and direct Presley as the dead star of an epic poem that smoulders with the aspirations and ashes of the twentieth century?' Geoff Dyer

'One of the most original virtuoso voices to be heard in the poetry of our fin de siècle' Lawrence Ferlinghetti

'Jeremy Reed's verse novel *Heartbreak Hotel* promises to be a great cult classic. It's a scintillating and exhilarating read. It's also devastatingly funny, truly stylish, and makes accessible, compulsive reading' Stephen Barber

'*Heartbreak Hotel* is a beautifully obsessive poetic exploration of Planet Elvis. It's a masterwork [...] Only Jeremy Reed, a supreme word-musician, could have created it' Adrian Mitchell

'Jeremy Reed is the real definition of British poetry now and deserves to be worshipped himself' Richard Hell

Also by Jeremy Reed

POETRY
Selected Poems
By The Fisheries
Nero
Engaging Form
Nineties
Red-Haired Android
Kicks
Pop Stars
Saint Billy

NOVELS
Blue Rock
Red Eclipse
Isidore
When The Whip Comes Down
Diamond Nebula
Chasing Black Rainbows
Dorian

BIOGRAPHY
The Last Star: Marc Almond
Another Tear Falls: Scott Walker
The Last Decadent: Brian Jones

HEART BREAK HOTEL

JEREMY REED

ORION

First published in Great Britain in 2002 by
Orion
An imprint of Orion Books Ltd
Orion House, 5 Upper St Martin's Lane,
London WC2H 9EA

A CIP catalogue record for this book is
available from the British Library

ISBN 0 75285 159 4

Typeset at The Spartan Press Ltd,
Lymington, Hants

Printed in Great Britain by
Clays Ltd, St Ives plc

For my mother, Lene, Moo and John,
with love

Contents

Foreword: The Biography of a Myth

How do you write the biography of a myth, the as-told-to kiss-and-tell chronicle of an angel? Jeremy Reed, the soul and body and anointed monarch of generosity, has found a way. He who has always written tributes to his small stable of personal stars – everyone from Billy Holliday to Marc Almond – has found a new means to write the life story of Elvis Presley. His method is not to start at the beginning unfolding Presley's life slowly and chronologically nor by building up the facts. Rather, he flashes on scenes in the singer's meteoric ascension and slow burnout of decline. He flashes on these moments so thoroughly that he inhabits them, invests them even, as an army can be said to finally 'invest' a fortress to which it has laid siege.

Jeremy Reed can hear, smell and touch the tacky gilded chambers that the King withdrew into, as Huysman's Des Esseintes withdrew into the artificial paradise of his enclosed rooms in the novel *A Rebours* or *Against the Grain*. Just as this archetype of the Decadent movement rarely stepped outside the controlled and aestheticised décor of his house, similarly Reed's Presley resides permanently in his hermetic chambers, watching the twin TVs he has had installed on the ceiling so that he won't have to sit up in bed to watch them. As he dozes, drugged, in Graceland, his passengerless Cadillacs are sent out on a tour as *ex votos* in a cult in which the deity is dead or dying.

Reed has an uncanny way of burrowing into each of these scenes (so kitsch they become tragic). Painted babydoll girl playthings are introduced into this permanently nocturnal world, and gangs of friendly layabout guys are always ready for food-fights or shoot-outs with their boss: it being understood that he will always gun them down. Yet, constantly haunting Elvis is the image of his dead mother Gladys, she who always believed in his talent and insisted that a Bethlehem-bright star hung over his birthplace. If Elvis runs out of constructive things to do, he can always dye his eyelashes again or sculpt his hair with a comb.

Although Reed has mastered Elvis's own dialect, he integrates it into a grander, more expressive language of his own devising, as if doing a hundred ever more virtuoso variations on a simple ten-note tune. Reed is Horowitz spinning out a finger-defying version of Chopsticks:

> He lives it all on overflight,
> the planet glimpsed as a blue cone.

The woman tumbling down the stairs
are a skirts-lifted waterfall.

That is Reed's condensed way of rendering the complexity of
Elvis's distance from the hysteria he creates wherever he goes.

Just as a bride is accompanied by a bevy of lovely maids, in the
same way Reed surrounds his chorus with a backup chorus of other
rock stars – Keith Richards, John Lennon, Jimi Hendrix – each of
whom lends the King one of his royal attributes: lyricism, sexual
drive, playfulness. Just as a king might be thought to be composed
of all his lands and castles, in the same way Elvis and his magic are
distributed over his cars, fans, and fantasies. In Reed's 'Golden
Legend of Elvis', the singer moves in a shadow cortège of phantom
Marilyns and James Deans. There is no time in Reed's world: no
development. There are only privileged moments that are at once
absolutely still and hysterically charged. In this world Elvis, even in
the 1950s, is already living by means of a strange kind of mystical
anticipation in the afterglow of Marilyn or Dean's death.

One of Elvis's most persistent appetites is for junk food and
Jesus. When he isn't sending letters to Our Lord he is ordering up
cheeseburgers folded into buns that have each been deep-fried in
half a slab of butter. Some of the funniest and most moving
poems bare titles like 'Elvis Eyes a Jam Donut' or 'Junk-food Junkie'
('The man's a cheeseburger mausoleum').

Reed is the English Rimbaud, the bad-boy of poetic innovation
and semantic shock tactics. With one difference: Rimbaud, in his
few brief years as a poet, was fiercely fashioning an image of him-
self as the Infernal Bridegroom, or as the vagabond back from
exotic places, cast-tanned and half-naked on the beach, whereas
Reed lives through his idols. He is an idolater and Elvis is the Baal,
the object of his one-man devotions.

Edmund White

PROLOGUE

Elvis Presley

He's photographed against a Cadillac,
one of the many littering his park,
white shoes conspicuous against the black

jacket, the cliff edges around the quiff
broken by gelled strands, loose diagonals.
His posture's always informally stiff,

it seems to say, 'I am the first and last
to make music into a religion.
My virtue is in owning to no past,

and yet the present leaves me obsolete.'
The antebellum façade at Graceland
has two stone lions guarding the retreat;

the rooms are kitsch, an ersatz movie set,
no sound, no light, and yet the *mise en scène*
describes the man: wall-to-wall mirrors vet

the ostentation without commentary.
A red room, blue room, chandeliers, peacocks,
each piece has no familiarity,

but suggests someone filling in a space
eclectically, obsessed by the unreal,
catching sight of himself in a surface

in which a sculpture preens. His fall was long,
cushioned by chemical supernovas.
We listen. Who is that inside the song?

ALL SHOOK UP

All Shook Up

The frisky ad-libber circles the mike,
a prankster start-stopping a buzz-refrain,

jocularly pitching bass to falsetto,
the voice coded with kiss-me-quick

importunings, chocolatey vocal cords
basking on velvet air cushions.

Chartreuse shirt, brand-name black Levi's,
he switches to a piano, jams

gospel solemnity, crowds on the Lord
as tangential to rock'n'roll,

redemptive password to his mama's heart.
He's out to lunch scatty with studio time,

prevaricating, picking up a song
and dropping it, as though the words don't fit

vocal imagining. He's left alone
to mix his colours from instinctual know,

naïve palette toned consummate finish.
His musicians noodle and tune

conspiratorially. The time wings by.
Without warning he loads into a take,

an unrehearsed live run, a give-it-all
no-limits-spared shamanic eloquence

that's almost there, one in the can, and one
to bring a generation to its knees.

The First Coming

Ball lightning chased across the stratosphere,
epic innuendos to a summer storm,
a swampy, fly-stuck, Mississippi clam,
quick orange feelers twitching the boondocks

before the hot frying-pan hiss of rain,
a couple racing through Overton Park
to tumble in a Lincoln, hair flattened
and sparkling with beady ionized drops.

The scene of first triumph, those snaky hips
electrifying every transfixed eye,
head down, and the involuntary sneer
meanly attitudinizing new youth –

gelled cliffhangers, guitars and bee-stung lips,
'That's All Right (Mama)' blazed across the air
like mainlined speed, a first-time knee-jerking
impetuously impromptu give all

to the immediately responsive crowd.
Glory was in the air; a pink rainbow
visible as a sign above massed oaks,
change and its leader vitalized the South.

He smooches Dixie inside the canned car,
the rain boiling off metal, it's so loud
it sounds like big boots trampling polythene.
She's half afraid. He's wired to a future

in which his messianic hype through rock
will leave him as the untouchable King.
The rain has tracked his hair over his eyes,
she almost wishes that he couldn't sing.

Sun Studios

Friday in downtown Memphis. Elvis slips
into Sun Studios; his blue suede shoes
are petulantly upfront like his lips.

His voice is feeling for its baritone
the way the Mississippi flows down deep;
he finds its colour on his hyoid bone.

Sam Phillips stands abashed. He can't control
the need to wonder at raw energy
shape-lifted as a ballad from the soul.

A hopped-up blues, Elvis sings white-boy black,
his gospel roots inflecting every note;
the sweat picks tunnels down his satin back.

Propulsive riffs, single-string filigree,
they get a slapback echo, feed on it,
while Elvis kicks in rhythm, and cuts free,

exuberantly wiring in his speed,
the voice of a new youth, a live attack
on dead conventions. Now his voice is freed

he hijacks tonal beat, and lays it down,
as though he's got the flavour of a mood
latent in every rebel over town.

It's the spontaneous rough take pulls it through,
'Blue moon of Kentucky', spoofed to a dazed
black country pop song, and each word sung true.

On the Road (1956)

Dust as the South's ubiquitous dry surf,
Arkansas, Nashville, a pink Cadillac
sidles with schmaltz ostentation across

a ranch-gapped landscape. When a tyre pops,
a mean hood in silver-spurred biker's boots,
his Clairol-black pompadour part-collapsed,

moons by the car, holding a teddy bear
won at a local carnival. They're late
to meet a bandshell show, and Elvis stares

wide-eyed into the blue Arkansas sky,
as though the moment's frozen for a shoot.
Two dumpling aides cowboy it into town,

pool-shooting moodies, they address a store
for clamshell-sized, fat-raddled hamburgers,
a bruised cholesterol sore oozing fat-cheese...

Elvis is junk-addicted. His first bite
eliminates a quarter pound. The clouds
are building to a concertinaed storm.

The rain slams in, but he stays on outside,
a mad, snake-hipped, contortionist dancer,
a sequined flash glitzing each trouser leg,

his rhythm bonded with the stereo,
as though he's his first and last audience,
there in Arkansas, singing in the rain.

Death Drive – James Dean

The desert blasts him with its tortured forms,
the landscape metaphoring sex
the way he likes it as human ashtray
with leather congeries. He feeds the car,
a silver Porsche Spyder, towards a red
eruptive sunset's glower,
a last receding coronal spotlight,
the hot air whipping at his white T-shirt
is speedy with chemical tang –
the fast evasive rip of being alive
as a subversive breakaway
zips through his energies – DHEA –
he's a rebel who fits the age
without his knowing why, just like the car
burns destiny along the scorching road.
The future roofs him like the sky
with amazingly conceived potential,
the dark dropping over the hills
like a cat burglar – he rotates the speed
from 70 to 85 and strips
the road in easy stages, starts to crowd
on overkill, hair scooped out by the wind,
his focus trained on the intersection,
a white Ford jabbing at his visual frame,
a lumbering 1950s hulk
equivocating at the Y-junction,
a rubber stamp of brakes, a second try,
his aim so suicidally head-on
it's like a dream in which he's paralysed,
the impact banging in his head
before it happens, feet bracing the floor,
the hurtled overreach detonating
simultaneous with blackout, every cell
fusing as instantaneous flash,
direct head-butt into the primal dark
in which he's disconnected, blown so far
he frazzles like a meteor
roaring on a trajectory through space.

Hayride Ecstatics

Bottoming out he clatters the pool cue,
mouth wide as a trout-ring
from boredom.
He's daytime phobic, so nocturnalized
he's dusted with dark like face powder.

The players are incidental,
faceless as black buttons on black.
They're accidental to his scheme,
a disappearing act, sex-fuses set,
predatory on the shark's leftovers…

He stories a country dog –
puts highlights in the narrative
the unextraordinary viewed from a car
given a name, the only meaning thing
in a week's bewildering virtual rush.

Stage-dressing's a two-hour ritual,
doing his hair makes inroads on ennui,
he's suddenly all he's got,
narcissistic about a wicked pimple,
learning to do thin-highwayed eyeliner.

Under the tent he's lasered,
the spotlight mooning a waist-down frenzy,
a speeded-up pelvic mania
like someone jump-starting a bike
twistedly hotseated with frustration.

His kicked-in dynamic's inaudible
against hysterical surf,
he's outdecibelled by teeny rampage,
the band grinding to abrupt halts
synchronized to when he stops dancing.

Untouchably autoeroticized,
he's Mr Twentieth Century
framed in dispensing religious heat
in ways so instinctual he's terrified,
praying for deliverance from the beat.

Gladys

She's like a lake or mountain. Permanent.
Her *Better Homes and Gardens Cookbook* bleeds
with fat-popped splotchy asterisks.
She mirrors every octave of my mood

from a James Dean lookalike blue
to gritty Memphis cool. Our bedtime talks
are intimate like lazy wasps

confiding in a boozy pear.
I tell her fame's a gold constellation
matching my lamé suit. I show her all

my Lansky's, Beale Street, clothing purchases,
a bolero jacket, a striped affair
watermarked with a black collar,
the paste jewels breezed on my compacted fist...

My mussed, and smoochily quixotic hair
gelled to a cliff-wall, tumbles at her hand.
She sits in a stained brocade dress,
ingenuously hidden from the fans
under the clumpish oaks that mob the drive,

and feeds her querulous chickens.
She's mother to me, in my gospelled blood,
her matrix deeper than the South's

swallowing on a continent.
She feeds me book-sized sandwiches,
the peanut butter raised like a doorstep,
its gravel crunching at my bite.

She's my elected valentine;
I can't outwalk her radius.
She stands there on the porch, hands on her hips,

and all the wide-eyed, Southern heavens shine.

Jesse

We're always doubles – one life for the two,
as though a walk-in touched my space
with fuzzy presence, fingerprinted time

and left a tremor on a piano key,
but couldn't stay. Planes disappear,
trains derail into parallel tunnels,

warps happen in the quantum foam.
I wonder sometimes if he's not reborn
and passes as a stranger in the street,

another quiffy Elvis lookalike
searching for a lost mother's hand,
a black-coated review of Lonely Street.

My absent twin walks through my inner house,
tries all the doors, but never shows.
His laughter's freaky with delay.

Once, there were footprints on a glass ceiling
an upside-down graffito's trick.
I sponged his out-there signature,

a snail's ectoplasmic glitter.
My stillborn brother's me when I'm on stage,
he flips my introversion inside out.

I mourn his closeness. Grief's a negative,
a lifetime soaking in the tray,
the image always low definition.

We'll meet each other the B-side
of life – he'll be my guardian at the end,
grabbing my hand to cross the one-way bridge.

Elvis Boogies with Liberace

It's raining stardust in the showman's hair,
the pianist's excess is Byzantine glitz,
extemporizing notes, his preenish smile
winning attention to his busy hands
glamming a sphinxy pink sapphire,

catwalking rings across the ivories.
Elvis assimilates this Zeitgeist dare.
The Venus Room has planet wall reliefs,
gold nebulae showered on magenta space.
The diners clatter plates industrially.

The pianist has 18-carat gold heels
and a mink finish to his gestural repertoire.
His groove is feminine. His eyelashes
flutter like wind lifting a pleated hem,
his audience tinkle along spinal nerves.

He boasts palatial gilt-on-white estates,
piano-shaped swimming pools, piano-shaped chairs,
drop-earrings clipped on fluted wineglasses,
gold satin sheets, hair buffed ten times a day,
a sybaritic discourse with glamour;

his bitchy repartee's a honey twist
on blackened toast, barbed campy one-liners
shredding the dress on dialogue.
His velvet suits are figure-caressed sleek
moleskin plumbago, thunderstorm-violet.

Elvis sips at the maestro's furnishings,
his bask in shimmer decadence.
They're like two emperors choosing one cloth
for peacocked rivalry, a gold-on-gold
race across red carpets to win the stage.

1034 Audubon Drive

A curvy asphalt lane, green tree-bobbed place,
Elvis invests in a bungalowed-heart,
a kitsched-up sanctuary, a Gladys roost,
a ladder above poverty
on which to hang red tinsel Christmas stars,
a cute mail-order-furnished artefact
earned by the black-boy fever in his blood,
the mantic R & B discourse
conducted with a lyric soul
loaded with gospelling blue archetypes.
Elvis has homed his energies
into suburbia, a high marriage
with middle values – the car says it all –
a Pepto Bismol-pink Crown Victoria
the glammy privilege of the laurelled star.
Venetian blinds, Formica, hi-fi sets,
a fifties sitcom-palace stagey bash
at flouncy furnishings proclaims the new,
the cushy and the soft-edged show
of being comfortable.

         E's scarlet phone
is hailed with rhinestones. His canary lamp
juts on a long neck like a crane;
his record sleeves are gloss-slewed on the bed.
His relatives camp on the lawn
itchy with magpied curiosity.
They carload into Memphis, sceptical,
raw-featured, driven by a hurried rain.

The cat's expected home.
               He leaves the train
east of the city limits at no stop
and makes slow tracks across an empty field
of burrs and foxtails, hayish grass,
his suit catching at seeds, and walks it home,

a clutch of records in one hand,
quizzative, head-bowed, reflecting on fame
and how his loneliness shines up like glass.

The Perfect Stranger (1956)

Slavonian Lodge, the Airman's Club, he's cruel
with looks so gorgeous that they kill
the shine on every girl rival's
attentioned eye-linered stand out

as kiss-and-dare wannabes, pouty teens
poured into jeans and pencil skirts
littering him with perfumed envelopes –
babydoll blondies pleading for a date,

letters written in pink lipstick.
He scans the crowd with rain-slick eyes,
the wooden chairs are schoolroomy –
300 hot seats dragged in from a shed,

and someone's sitting in his glow
before he knows it, feels the vibrant pull
into her concentration-field,
the recognition building song by song

to eye contact, her smile opening
the way a morning glory reads the sun
in costume changes, blue to pink,
her hopes squirrelling in a girlfriend's ear

as he returns her smile direct,
then goes down possessed to the grainy boards,
no other contact but a mike
between him and explosive energies…

He's singing to her now, so flash
and virtuosic, she's aware
of live connections, bites her hand
and grabs at his posed, shoulders-raised profile…

Then backstage in the break, back to the wall
he's diffidently looking out
for her to join him, and she's June,
surfing to meet him on a curvy board.

Mama's Got Her Eyes on You

The thumb unzips a single line of peas,
little commuter queue in bright-green skins,
their rotund bodies flipped into a bowl

are convexed to a rising watermark,
a jostled sheen with black warps showing through...
Gladys spins the bowl like a steering wheel

and eyes the leather duds, the shelled-out husks.
June's nerves are filigree: her inner noise
is steady downpour. Elvis curls a lip

and dances out to the red telephone.
June's voice goes missing under scrutiny
and holidays in an off-limits zone.

It's kick-pleats break the tension. June's neat seams
and hemline stitching win a mutual storm
of seamstress interchanges. Blue thread, red,

Gladys finds no tripped stitch and compliments
her son's glam finding, who is leggily
arranged, pea-popping in a cobalt chair.

Elvis is flirting with a teenie-cat
from Lauderdale who cliff-edges his hair.
June's ears glower as though they're hiving bees.

Gladys cuts ship-prows of coconut cake
from a round gravestone, and the flaky grains
are finger-stubbed by Elvis at a whisk.

HOUND DOG

Hound Dog

His vocal attack chops the rumba beat,
he tilts the mike stand, pushing it away
like a shadow-projection of himself –

a sculptural flower cut from the abdomen,
a pivot to emotional build, collapse,
wrists splayed out, arms wide, head defiantly

chewing the rhythm, presenting sideways,
the face turned downwards, then the figure thrown
into a backwards spine-curved overreach,

before the forward lurch carries his feet
right to the sea's edge of imploring hands
working to grab at a frenzied blue shoe…

He scoops his hair without a finger-flick,
just pours it back in motion, hardly knows
the cutting-edge he crosses with each twist

of gender violation, checked jacket
too roomy on the shoulders, velvet-cowled,
his legs jackknifing to a triangled

seam-splitting provocation, attitude
written in every gesture, as he tries
another spontaneously improvised

pelvic gyration, drags the microphone
right to the floor, spirals up, points a hand
in half-time, and freezes on the last note.

He's All Hesitations

A pre-fame Friday afternoon,
blowzy, bluesy, nothing-to-do
times, buying flowers for Mom
and fluttery over right choice
of colourful extravagance –
hot redhead roses winningly
plump in his arms, his first-time try
at black mascara on the street
attentioning hostility,

he's restively, introspectively,
courteously shy,
a long time from another blue Friday,
Jerry Lee Lewis shouting at shut gates –
Presley's a faggoty hair-dyed
King of pubescent Lolitas
a subject for the underworld's
black pack dogs, for the slink-eyed wolf,
the drunk raver dragged off by police.

Leiber/Stoller

Fifties hip tailoring – the studio photograph
MGM 1957
professes obligatory bespoke suits,
slimline black ties, the popster songwriters
bonding their white-boy-black-blood R & B
impulse dynamic with a wired Elvis
lifting back from the sheet music

in a moment's insightful discovery
as though connecting with the mains
like biting at an orange.
They're citified New Yorkers, sceptical
of E's untutored punkishness.
Stoller has one brown eye, one blue,

and manics ideas like he's playing squash
with run-on lines.
Mike partners E in playing four-hand blues
at the grand piano. Stoller sings.
Their reservation warms as current jabs
into a common feeling. E's red shirt
is splashy like a poppy. He's all dare

and courteous temerity
taking the chocolate wrapper off their songs
and placing toothmarks in the words.
They've scored the theme for *Jailhouse Rock*,
reluctantly, locked in a hotel room
to page their boppish energies –
Coke bottles littering a smokestacked cram.

Jerry conducts with body English,
while E persists in worrying new takes
to load the can. They're photographed history,
intensely concentrated into time
and thumbprinted on analogue,
the two songwriters talking shop on floor,
no other interests, jerky on caffeine,
a fazed producer throwing up his arms
and in blue temper heading for the door.

Kingdom

The Lizard-King, the Pentecostal cat,
the orphic celebrant in black Levi's,
Elvis retrieves the legendary blueprint
from storage in a pile of shirts

at Lansky's, the brightest silk ruck.
He hesitates outside the store,
afraid, the hot flush turning cold,

the street tilting to forty-five degrees,
then righted as he straightens out
back to a wall, as though he's frisked
from shoplifting identity
for godhead weird as finding a red rose

growing from graffitied concrete,
a rose so dark its reds are black.
The tree of life opens along his spine,

gateways him with the early dead.
He straps himself inside his car,
chosen, but angular to how
youth notches forty summers on the vine

before lightning consumes the plant.
He'll never now escape death's gates,
the angel waiting at the terminal,
gold mouse charged by a gold touchslate,
the programme holographed EP.

He drives home, and his vision's clear,
his face describes the century's
provocative youth-cultured sneer;
he practises a crooked pouting smile
and freezes the perversity.

He's certain now, and the Las Vegas lights
neon his vision – all those pinks and golds
writing his name in virtuality.

Burning a Pink Cadillac

The road's on warped linear time-release,
it dulls by repetition, wipes out clear
adjustments to the moment.

                         They're down South;
cumulus-bangs building all afternoon
to a mauve auditorium,
a sticky, June thunder-premonition,
oppressive clingfilm heat coating the skin,
Elvis cradling a Coca-Cola can,
flaked out from last night's hotspot jackknifed thrust
to win a hometown audience,
twitches his toes in pink socks, feels the car
make wide-screen takes on the skyline, then blow
to a brake-flattened roadside halt,
abrupt as cardiac arrest,
no detonative impact, but black smoke
volcanoing upfront, the car on fire,
their quick hands jettisoning instruments,
ejecting cases, as they run for clear
and watch the limo crumple into flames,
a blue and orange surfing roar
sheeting the bodywork, a fast attack
of ripping conflagratory energies
roofing the car's gutted interior,
the molten construct collapsed on itself,
auto-cannibalized atrocity
spitting itself out as black ash.

                               They stand,
roadsided, almost joined in prayer,
E's first pink Cadillac funeralled at noon,
there on the road between Hope and Texarkana,
big stadiumed clouds standing off, and the smoke

subsiding, as they start to run
in mad hilarity around an oak.

Fireworks Fight

A dusty hill site tree-screened from the road.
Elvis wears a blue jumpsuit, goggles, gloves,
combat gear, as the teams split Red and Blue
for warring territorial rights,
a pyrotechnical shoot-out,
the Memphis gang become incendiaries,
blazing each other off the trail in smoke
fogging the dusty auditorium,
a reeking gunpowdered occlusive cloud
tenting combatants, smudging a membrane
over a blue chiaroscuro
of figures taking up the fight for real.
A conflagratory extravaganza
of torchy Roman candles, firecrackers
skyrockets, niggerchasers, baby giants,
five thousand dollars' worth of touchpaper
hurtled to near-miss body-aim,
Elvis has wacked somebody on the boot
and got a glancing shoulder blow.
He rampages for Blue, guerrilla crawls
out of a stumpy bush, then zigzags close
to where a Red combatant's sprained a knee,
but keeps on firing from a squat.
The air is punchy with their raucous screams,
the mad hilarity of thrust
and counterthrust, an arsenal consumed
in sixty minutes' undercover sham
hostilities. Somebody's in-the-face
unnerving firecracker is deflected
on its whizzy purple trajectory
and gloved over a shoulder.

                                    It's an end.
Elvis signals a pyrrhic victory,
loosens his helmet, and the embers cook
in snuffled drags of churlish smoke.
The mob troop back to limos, back to town,
Elvis's hair turbaned in a pink towel,
his anger silenced, and his foot tapping
to some girlie group number's poppy hook.

Elvis Does Bubblegum

It's oral rumination
this rubbery teat-blowing
feat, stretching a pink
onion-shaped cupola
like the opalescent crisis
pearling in a condom,
a Schiaparelli shocking
architectonics
shape-sculpted by the tongue
to an impacted bubble
deflated after showing.
Elvis fast-tracks and slow-tracks
the metamorphosis,
signals a groove,
then alters the rhythm.
The flavour's bleached out
from midsummery berry
to a tongue-rollered ennui
stringily taste-hoovered,
hinty with synthetics.
His mafia all do it
as lip-synced calisthenics,
orchestrated air-bubbles
pinking in vacant mimetics.
E's the provocative leader
of the fish-mouthed ensemble
pouting sugary vowels
as though they're tubular,
air bubbles pinging
on a baize-still lake.
The big one's translucent
like an aquarium
or helicopter cockpit,
or a space-rigged dome.
It's the cracklish dénouement
to a group afternoon,
the applause at the break
more for the expertise
of stretching a membrane
to a perfect fit.

Uh-huh

Shivery intonation
like playing frets along the spine
does the listener over
uh-huh uh-huh
and you're mine

An autographed lavender
Lincoln Premier
crawled over with names
uh-huh uh-huh
lipstick games

A real-sweat pink shirt
kited from a window
shredded in an alley
uh-huh uh-huh
make it hurt

A Billboard entry
vocal Kundalini
slinky velvet
uh-huh uh-huh
has you flirt

'I Got a Woman'
gut-sung with closed eyes
down deep in a dark space
uh-huh uh-huh
it's all lies

Lawdy a tone
like Virginia creeper
triggering longing
uh-huh uh-huh
you're alone

Licking the gloss
off a black-and-white photo
signed on the lips
uh-huh uh-huh
what a loss

A sharp-hipped cat
with a funky mind-set
giving it his all
uh-huh uh-huh
no regret

Sing to make women
let down their hair
unpin it in the car
uh-huh uh-huh
what a star

HOUSE OF THE RISING SUN

The Vanities

Defrosting purple vanities,
it's childhood he remembers, sweet
grievance on an empty plate,

car tyres killed flat and no repair.
Jewelled encrustations on his shirt,
he recollects a patched-up state,

mother crying for poverty.
Manicured in a private jet
under a king-size bed's red coverlet,

his memory returns to cold
blue fingers on blue afternoons,
childhood Decembers scripting frost

as sparkle in a jeweller's tray.
Aggrandized as the chosen one
he reads in anonymity

soluble freedom that he's lost.
Crowded out of solitude,
stadiumed like a Reichstag fling,

it's a pubescent loneliness,
an acned leave-me-alone phase
he nurtures like the sound of rain.

Discredited for ballroom slams,
a cocktail hour Las Vegas drawl,
it's punking a packed airman's club

brings measure to his tedium
in looking back – two jackets to his name –
the pilots joking in the wooden bar.

House of the Rising Sun

A deep, bluesy lament rolls through my blood,
a message from the underworld
storied into a grainy voice

panning for gold inside a whisky shot,
a folky way of treating guilt
as something written on the door
that's inerasible, a sign

bar coded
into consciousness. Nina Simone
smokes the song out of a blue hole
to reinvest the ruined youth
with tear-choked, drop-dead-soon remorse,

the unredeemed bar-crawler lost for good...
My barn carries the ballad's name,
a lightning-nerved, ponderous horse questions
the burnished walls, a risen sun
glowering with thunder in its vaulted heart:

it dreams of sunstorms, meteors,
the gold membrane over a lake
sheened like a sunset in a glass of wine.

The song celebrates how a shame
lives like a patch on every heart;
a youthful tear that never heals,
a seam no red thread stitches tight

on the divide.
I play it, and I'm ten again
in Tupelo, and Gladys runs
to find me in a raffish clump

of sumacs, where dark sexual mysteries hide.

Cherry Tart

Memphis is Presley's point in time.
Malarial swamps. Red bruised-up trucks.

Millennial supercomings. Mosquitoes
type in apocalyptic prophecies;
the one in rhinestones calling in the lost

from violent highways. A black sun

balanced on an oversized knee.
Crowned from the freezer, cherry tart

is a cool, squishy sugar-feed.
The mouth will open like a gothic arch
for quick appeasement,

continuous need.
Prophets visit patisseries,

sensitize chakras, ride in gold limos
towards an altar in the wind,

their white suits sometimes stained by cherry tart.

Gospel

It's bottom note and top; body and soul.
It bumps his skin like goose pimples
bringing the Lord back home again

to sit on a black Beckstein lid.
The music cooks in him like coffee beans.
It tastes of longing, doorwayed in the rain.

Sister Rosetta Tharpe's his role model,
flame-haired corona shot from poverty
to a silk-nyloned stadiumed apogee...

It's dignity learned from humility
lives in his breath control. It's planing wood
and loving cow-eyed knots found in the grain.

It's his first contact in the studio,
basing himself in comfort repertoire,
having the empty spaces in him sing.

It's learning black in a white skin,
working means singing when the odds are stacked
against survival. Words pour as a chant

and vertically. Redemption's in that praise.
It's first hearings; a boy awake at night
quizzing voices from a neighbouring window

and finding ways to re-create the tone.
It's body language, breath for breath a scale
of squeezing tightest cares like orange pips.

The Colonel's Machinations

The blindside man. Rumbustious,
ex-fairground, entrepreneurial whizz,
cigar-stoppered bark, bellicose
PR belligerent hit-bulk
of Elvis management.
Stipulator of non-negotiable
winner-takes-all contractual rights,
his scrunched fedora's seated back
as though impacted there, green mash
of unattended felt.
He's real-lifed from a gangster film,
moon-faced crude rube, monogamous
to his creation, nowhere man,
no roots, no past, no history,
just Elvis starlit on his mind
as godspeak. Wacky in his groove
he's a jocular snow dealer,
a paunchy lumbering bison
kneeling on violets where they grow,
his whiphand always undertoned.
His ways clear forests at a swipe,
old huckster dug up from the South
to network for the blinding new
with mock affection for hot property
and quizzed amusement at his sell.
The incongruities marry,
the seasoned and naïve death-trip
towards a Hollywood gold bowl
lined with blue diamonds. He's admonitory,
keeps Elvis islanded inside Graceland,
non-contributive to biography…
His hold's a strangulating python's grip,
a breath-squeezed-out paralysis.
Elvis gets flattened, damp-mooded,
dispirited and learns by rote
a silent acquiescence, dubs his will
to Thom's despotically crash oversee,
his threats track-listed from a gun
concealed inside his mind, the safety catch
half on, half off, the sights lensed on EP.

Interiors Fetish

Elvis keeps colouring his hill-site dream,
he thinks the house will dematerialize
if he's away too long, his mind
draw blank on the antebellum façade,
white fronting columns, a stage-set
teleported out of *Gone with the Wind*,

grand Georgian mode facelifted in Memphis,
build Furbringer and Ehrman, 1938.
His mood switches with the decades
from indigo-cobalt interiors,
companioned in depth-tones by claret piles,
to white and gold, high contrast reds
sunsetted in satin armchairs,
loud, glitzy statements of the rhinestone-king
equalling every fantasy
with its external counterpart; mirrors,
red velvet drapes, gold leather couch,
gilded dentilation, ivory piano,
and crushed mother-of-pearl gold bedroom door.
The house is mother: it's stability,
as though Gladys has never really left
her kitchen sanctuary, and prompts the change
to green shag carpeting, and fussy lamps.
Elvis extemporizes drag
in every flourish given to the place,
the glitzy indoors waterfall, the camp
attention to sequined detail.
His big cat's lair is gold and black and red,

a mausoleum to a dead mother
he squeezes like an orange in his heart
to drain the memories, and up all night
communicates his sense of loss
to an indifferent house, and feels her near
as energies twitching his spine,
and in a dark place throwing on a light.

Elvis's Neckties

Are slinkily fancy
things, a white knit
a scarlet
knitted flick
anorexically skinny

sixties sartorials,
black or blue leather
chisel-blunt square
stringily slimline
testimonials

to starstruck couture.
Or polka-dot pink
in fattish satin,
kipperish, smackish
shaped to a point,

sheened ostentatious
a twenties bash
at bouncing off a shirt
a dark green and orange
muddled loud sunset.

Later abandoned
for Napoleonic collars
the five-inch-collar builder
worn to see Nixon
tieless for effect.

Or a classic black tie
presumed morbid
a thunderstorm black
worn in strict contrast
to a sunny mood.

Elvis's Pets

A loopy fracas in the chicken-run,
a raucously scrawny redcrest
gobbles with an overcrammed craw

then stomps it like a territorial bull,
a cock with flashing red temper
harried by Gladys to a cowering cringe

of flattened machismo.
Five donkeys in the disused swimming pool
drowse with innate passivity

on straw mopped over egg-blue tiles.
Back of the house stabled lightning
is a stomach-knotted gold horse

nerves pitched like a Stradivarius
paused for a thunderous scherzo.
Elvis is horse-dimensioned: cool with it

and wired to a love of speed.
Indoors an irate monkey pushes weights,
dressed in a satin cowboy shirt

and hoppily cavorts across the room
with a red handbag on his arm,
firing a raunchy-phrased soliloquy.

The peacocks vamping sea-blues in the drive
peck finish off gloss limousines
and leave a scratch graffiti on preened doors.

It's All Over Now, Baby Blue

I see her chickens gobbling pan-fried corn,
and her so simple, touching life like that,
or pocketing for me a gold acorn,

a woody top I'd pressure in my hand
as the impacted blueprint of a tree.
She's dying of the pills I understand

as the new alphabet surrounding fame.
Her bourbon empties are accusing things,
cold witnesses to a nocturnal game

she played in secret, and with me away.
Girls eyebrow-plucked each grass-blade on the lawn,
or spooned sachets of dust. She'd have them stay,

her rural hospitality so sure
in little ways of earthing the starstruck
they'd feel my roots planted deep in nature.

Our lives were shattered by revelation,
my messianic starburst shining through
as soul-charge activating a nation,

an instantly bright happening. I feel
her system shutting down, her fuses blown,
the damaged places that I cannot heal.

She's my first love and last. I hear her call
my name, as though she's drowning in a pool
turned white with thunder from a waterfall.

Elvis Sees Jesus

Between two interfacing cloud-banks, sun,
a hazy-eyed nimbus, then big-shot glower,
a red eruptive planetary thump

transmitting energies. A bus-lagged group
deal cards for Elvis on the desert road.
He's fazed out, but star-profiled, born to win

despite the setbacks. When the light shines through
he snaps on dark glasses – it's cool that way –
he's Marlon Brando pulled from the deep freeze.

The journey's rhythm, like the road's his pulse.
He can't get off it, and picks a guitar
to hear the discourse in him start to speak.

The miles wack by as reverb, sonic daze.
The scenic jump-frames break up and re-form
His spine feels scraped by a violinist's bow.

He's sighting nothing in a dusty sky,
splitzer-pink alto-cirrus, then a face
singles him out between clouds, studied pour

of concentrated energies, a flash
connecting with millennia in his soul,
a Jesus-wish to step out on the road

and be proclaimed, lift one arm to the sun
and know the power that thrills through every star
and codes the helix inside DNA.

Hall of Gold

It's like the gold room of an Inca king;
a blinding, sunstormed, incremental blaze,
a wall-to-wall glass-cased precinct
in which my mausoleumed trophies burn
a gold and platinum disc glory-trail;

the prototypical rock King's
auric halo translated into shine,
a validated showbiz aggrandizement –
gold lamé, gold records, gold Cadillacs,
the mystic gold-spot sweating on my skin…

Gene Vincent, Buddy Holly, and James Dean,
they had their gold skins split open by crash.
Their legend lives on, as eponymous
precursors of my Memphis legacy,
the snake-hipped bacchant acting cruel and mean.

The Word made Flesh. I got to earth that way.
My gold room is my feedback tomb,
I slouch there, moody in my biker's boots,
contemptuous of fame, but needing it
the way a smack-head mainlines a scored vein…

I hoard my Grammies, memorabilia,
my records written up as passing facts
go millions, teenage-based across the globe,
the E-arrival in a pink jacket
kicking a slapback sound to fifties youth,

and staying as the archetypal punk,
turned valentine, pacing a burnished room,
afraid to live, and terrified to die,
the old mortal dilemma, while the crowds
hang on the gates to breathe in the same air.

Cars

My kitschy, ostentatious autocade –
a glitzy all-American graveyard
of elephants brought to a Southern rest.
My Lincolns, Cadillacs, the sexual thrill

of sniffing masculine interiors,
voluminous, concave leather ballrooms,
leaving the imprint of a lover's hand

as customized upholstery.
I'd give my cobalt hair a punkish quiff
in the wing mirror, catch my look
and hold it as a stormy take

on unrepentant youth.
My '56 grape-purple Cadillac,
nursed on the Memphis highways, smelled of fame

worn like a designer scent,
too briskly new to settle, but alive
to an intransigent America
miked-up to a pelvic Snake King.
Its purple carpets absorbed grape Kool-Aid.

Others, I loved, my Cadillac Fleetwood,
sprayed pink for Gladys, and my Stutz Blackhawk,
18-carat gold-plated trim
having the car shine like a royal tomb,
a King's red leather catafalque.

I'd burn the highways, getting off on speed,
my boot-black Dino Ferrari
tilting up on a manic trajectory,
a blonde beside me, all red pout
and attitude, lifting black wraparounds

to take in something modern, happening by,
a scrambled moment breathed into my ear,
her exclamation issued as a cry.

Love Lack Substitutes

Sultrily leggy aficionados,
they clone detail right to a shampoo flounce

and seem sweet temptation like chocolate mousse
compliant to a quick-dip spoon.

They're a drop-dead-gorgeous convocation,
a girlie Revlon-faced harem

assembled for foyer protocol,
the pre-selected and the try-it-ons.

Some get admitted to his suite
to sit beside the narcoleptic King

embalmed and bible-pondering,
avuncular to a belle's ivory

sleek second-figured negligée.
She lies beside him coffined, taut,

no least chance to be sinuous
to his imagined satyriasis.

He's respectfully circumspect.
She's there to mother his nocturnal drift,

complacent, passive, supervised,
the temptress showing from her cups,

shocked into effigial dormancy,
cold-toed, confused, and awake half the night.

Writing a Novel in Rock'n'roll

The corn-blue kid scratchcards every detail
of surface glitter, reads it right,
the way the big fish jump small, and the small
leap straight from Beale Street to Times Square
glittering with ingenuous
smalltown naïveties, lip-curled

with racy vision, and a trust
in the spontaneous as first and last
the true directed energy.
He'll point it up to a gold star

attendant on his everything.
Elvis at RCA New York
dressed in a lilac ribbon shirt
makes a pink snowball of his bubblegum

then tongues it to a diaphanous teat,
a vowel-shaped faux pas, threadily
contracting like a pink-horned snail
into a middle-mouth resignation.

He trips over his fork at lunch,
unsure of left hand, right hand etiquette,
his butch-waxed front hair falling down
like black spaghetti on his confusion,
his manners so polite, they smell of grass…

Later they walk out through the rain
fuzzing over Madison Square Garden,
a rain that smells of Sunday afternoons
and tired leather, a commentary
on fifties ennui, coffee bars,
and what it means to wait for the big light

to power through – he knows it all
how genius breaks rank, jumps the crowd to catch
the second bounce of a green tennis ball.

Come So Far

The morning glory's blue balletic poise,
no overreach, translucently
filigrees in October shine.
He's in their moment, but fast-forwarded

on a demagnetized trajectory,
no time to fingerprint discoveries,
or sit a hectic sunset out
with dotty bugs pixellating the porch.

He lives it all on overflight,
the planet glimpsed as a blue cone.
The women tumbling down the stairs
are a skirts-lifted waterfall.

Head slanted, left arm thrown out of the car,
dust burnt into his pores, he crosses
the desert like that once, a visionary
delirious with exhaustion and fire,

his driver aimed direct into the sun…
He's used inside so many heads
obsessed with image, that he's everywhere
present in someone's consciousness,

a clone coded on mental film.
He's somewhere, and a hummingbird
sips at a radial passionflower
injecting pansy colours as it dips

across his vision. He lifts biker's boots
on to support, and lives it through
time off from time, three minutes' solitude
like raindrops scoring notes in a wineglass.

HEARTBREAK
HOTEL

Heartbreak Hotel

Circa 1956. The building's lit by dark blue neons at the end of Lonely Street. Elvis sits moodily on the bonnet of a pink Cadillac parked outside the hotel's entrance. His cliffhanging, butch-waxed hair has collapsed over his eyes. He is wearing a pink jacket, tight black pants, and scuffed blue alligator loafers. He's the personification of the song's moody, atmospherically disquieting lyrics, the recording's overlay of echo and upbeat despair giving him a defiant, sultry, unrequited lover's image. He wants to be James Dean, but he's Elvis.

He's come so far in two years, and Memphis is still his indigenous location. The blue star which Gladys and Vernon legendize as having shone over the two-room shack in Tupelo, on the night of his birth, has turned gold. He is the acclaimed King. The Lizard King, the dionysian, prototypical rock star. It's purely inspirational. When he comes on at Tampa, Jacksonville or Las Vegas he runs directly to the microphone. His twenty-minute frenzy is abrupt, unrehearsed, phallocentric. He will hystericalize 'It's All Right', 'Blue Suede Shoes' and 'Hound Dog' and lean dejectedly into the agonized, self-immolative narrative of 'Heartbreak Hotel'. Legs spread wide apart, inhabiting a three-minute stillness under the spot, the song brings about a radical metamorphosis of his live act. In the course of singing it, he is already inhabiting posthumous fame. He knows the story of how the songwriters Mae Axton and Tommy Durden had composed the song after reading the story of a man who had committed suicide and left a note saying, 'I walk a lonely street.' He is already there. His mood is introspectively coloured indigo.

A blonde sashays out of Heartbreak Hotel. She wears a fitted red sequined cocktail skirt, and unnervingly high heels. She sips at her pouting femininity. She says to him, her red fingernails bleeding in five polished mirrors on his collar, 'I'm the ghost of Marilyn Monroe. I'm acquainting myself with death, so that when it happens, I'm prepared. That's why people come to this place. You must go inside too, and learn these mysteries. The desk clerk will show you the way to a room at the interior. Jimmy Dean is here regularly. You'll find him at the bar. He'll die soon. You'd better come in, and get acquainted with the place.'

Elvis follows Marilyn to the foyer. Dry ice smokes on the inside. He involuntarily gets out a comb and checks his hair. He can hear strains of himself singing 'Heartbreak Hotel'. Marilyn walks ahead with a pronounced gluteal wiggle. There are rhinestone tears splashed on the foyer mirror. He turns his collar up, and disappears into the wall of vaporized smoke.

Blue Suede Shoes

Elvis won't ever repair the pane of cracked glass at Graceland which Gladys fell through on the day before she was taken to the Methodist Hospital in Memphis, where she died. The fissure in the window, an elongated radial star, is like the breakage in his nerves. When he thinks of her, he falls into a corresponding jagged hole. It's she who always inculcated in him an absolute sense of self-belief. Even while he was driving a truck for Crown Electric in Memphis, she never lost sight of his difference from others, his innate gravitation towards stardom. And she nurtured the pockets of missing time in which he would just reflect on himself in the mirror, backcombing his hair with three separate preparations like a girl. It was Gladys who conspired with him on his first androgynous clothing purchases, a bolero jacket and a mauve ribbon shirt from Lansky's. And when in 1956 he bought her her first real home, a green rancher with black shutters and a tiled grey roof at 1034 Audubon Drive in Memphis, it was a confirmation of an inseparable familial bond.

The King stands backstage at CBS's Studio 50 between Fifty-third and Fifty-fourth, before appearing on the Dorsey Brothers' *Stage Show* in 1956. His imperturbable outer cool is a persona. He's already adopted a weirdo cult as an entourage. He kneads a sparkling mosaic of rhinestones in a closed fist. It's the empty kudos of being a star that attracts him to the kitsch approbation given his work. There's a total unreality to it like the stuffed animals scattered around his home: tigers, monkeys, bears, dogs, panthers, leopards. He doesn't know what to do, when the power isn't running through him. When he went out cold on overdrive, a doctor had told him that he consumed more energy in twenty minutes than a labourer would in eight hours. And the anticlimax is devastating. It's like running out of gas on the highway, nobody around for as far as the eye can see and go on seeing.

Mostly he succeeds by a punkish assault on the audience, his energized rush disarming their preconceptions of what pop music comprises. 'Baby, Let's Play House' is done as a storm, his hands twitching in frantic rhythm, and when they come to the instrumental break in each number he withdraws into the protective shelter of the band, spreads his legs wide, and lets rip. But again, it's what to do after he's burnt the adrenalin. He suffers a form of abject de-apotheosization. Gladys has taught him to sing hymns, but he connects somewhere else, with the cultic practices which are to become known as Elvisism, and the ritual of the sequined pentagram.

He bunches into a red jacket. Already he has outsold any other RCA artist on the Billboard charts. He picks up his customized leather-lined guitar and prays with his chords. He can feel the whole Mississippi flowing through his spine.

Last Train to Memphis

The bathroom carpet's a deep red. The black toilet's faced by a purple sink built into a marble counter. A mirror constellated with oversized coloured bulbs runs along the wall at counter length. A death-room, an inner sanctum, the intimate court of the hieratic King, a convention of teddy bears hold conference in the loose arrangement of velvet armchairs. The investigative team have broken the seal on his absence. If it's really him on his way to the big empty room, then his bluely discoloured body is in the emergency room at the Baptist Memorial Hospital in Memphis. The doctors have administered three shots of Epinephrine and two shots of Isuprel in the attempt to stimulate the heart. They've also performed a thoracotomy, an incision on the left side of the chest, and inserted a tube between the fourth and fifth ribs with the objective of reinflating a collapsed lung. They know Elvis is dead, but they go through the emergency procedures. One of them can see him watching on the other side; his etheric body is chased by a prismatic aureole. In the place where his heart was, there's a trembling butterfly.

At Graceland, the rooms sealed off from the relentless dog day, with its lifelessly oppressive heat, the investigation is failing to come up with evidence of drug samples to reinforce findings of forensic pathology. Elvis's personal black bag with its complement of tiny black plastic drawers inside, is empty. Someone has cleaned up so there are no vestiges of his prescription drugs in the bathroom or bedroom. No sign even of the drugstore analgesics he used so liberally. There are guns everywhere. A turquoise-handled Colt .45, a logo-engraved Python 357 pistol, an M16 fully automatic assault rifle, a pearl-handled Derringer, all the weaponry of someone fetishistic about the collection of firearms. The bedroom and the bathroom are looking for him. Objects are becoming depersonalized, they are no longer peculiarly animated by their owner's vibrational charge, they are reverting to a purely decorative and tacky clutter. His close aides can feel this. It's the first clear specifics of his death. Elvis's last live-in girlfriend, Ginger Alden, is constantly checking her clothes and make-up in the apprehension of the inevitable paparazzi. The people assembled in Elvis's bedroom have the air of house-breakers. They can't really believe they are there. The intrusion seems an unforgivable transgression. The book he was reading at the time of his death, *Sex and Psychic Energy* has had its cover turned back, so that the title's not visible.

There's a train passing through Memphis, they can hear it out by the boondocks near the airport. A blues train, carrying a passenger whose only luggage is the guitar he cradles on his lap. This train isn't stopping. Its windows are blacked out. It emits a long ululating scream and picks up speed headed south. The passenger looks back once, and begins picking out chords. Now he will sing.

Burning Light

Elvis likes to powder his face with stardust. Who are the great precedents in decadence? Heliogabalus, Nero, Antinous, Louis XIV, Marcel Proust's friend de Montesquieu, Oscar Wilde? Elvis's life has become a glam parody of Huysmans' *fin de siècle* compendium of pathologies *Against Nature*. His bright-red mynah bird flickers on to his outstretched arm. None of the Graceland staff are permitted to tell him what time it is, unless he has an urgent professional appointment. He no longer lives in real time. His IC costume company jumpsuits are exhibited on the walls like hundreds of simulacra of the King. They have all been given names, such as Inca Gold Leaf, Sundial, Burning Flame, Blue Aztec, Mad Tiger, American Eagle, Red Lion, King of Spades, and Blue Rainbow. He conserves every item of memorabilia, converting his mansion into a premature funeral chamber. The Egyptian god Anubis also wears blue suede shoes, and watches Elvis with inquisitive curiosity from his parapsychological dimension. He knows they will meet on his terms. He will hold up a mirror to Elvis, and the latter will see himself as someone else; the appointed one. The halls of the dead are also mirrored like the spiral staircase at Graceland.

Elvis rarely thinks without consultation. He doesn't trust all those loose connections on display in his mind. When Gladys was alive, he would wake her at any hour of the night if he felt troubled about problems rising on him. With the Memphis Mafia, the boys who are always on duty in the house, Red West, Sonny West and Dave Hebler, it's different. Their camaraderie is founded on a Memphis upbringing, an indigenous solidarity which presents its own simple values to a world which brings its adulation to the gates at Graceland. In the long periods of inertia between tours, the concentrated periods of reclusion which he increasingly cultivates, the King sometimes sprays his skin gold to complement his gold lamé shirt or gold pyjama trousers. His dysfunctional biochemistry no longer even responds to Dexedrine as a stimulant. His method of taking pills is aleatory. He will risk taking anything which seems a viable option to blunting the confusion which builds like static in his mind. He wants only to sleep and be free of colonic pain.

But there were times when he was burning light. When Gladys would sit outside Graceland, dipping snuff, and feeding the chickens, and he would remember the first pure visitations of the power investing him with a new form of music. She understood without him having to explain anything. He just had it, white light in his veins. White shoes, white belt and black pegged pants. Freedom was the flash of a wing on his shoulder. He sips at the retrieved light of 1954 and 1955. It's like a drinking straw siphoning memory, light so clear it fills the curtained room with sunrise.

Cadillacs

From a battered black Lincoln, cruising Beale Street and Union Avenue, the King graduates in May 1955 to a first pink and white Cadillac, his name painted in black on the door. It's like the acquisition of something externalized from a dream, a symbol transferred from one dimension to another. Cars smell of puberty, melon sliced into orange canoes on a plate, and they afford him a sense of feeling centred in life, as though the steering wheel represents a commitment to living. Elvis likes to dress for his pink Cadillac in a Kelly green suit. He flops against the kerbed limo, communicating with it as part of the Great American Dream. He is already dreaming of the customized models which will come to constellate the grounds of his future mansion. Elvis would like to name one of the near planets Gold Cadillac. Cars resonate with mythopoeic overtones in his mind. They are archetypes belonging to apocalypse. He likes the tactile qualities of fitting his body to coercive leather, and he's obsessed with chrome finishings, vectored wing mirrors, and the Hollywood connotations implied by ostentatious cars.

Flip to June 17, 1955, and he's standing on the road somewhere between Hope and Texarkana, watching his first Cadillac crumple into impacted flame, after a wheel bearing has caught fire. The sky's a solid blue block, it's indifference framing his distraught figure, as an alphabet of chokingly toxic smoke spirals up from the conflagration. He reads it as a warning. Someone has to drive a Crown Victoria down to his rescue so that he can fulfil a date in Dallas. He evaluates this reproachful admonition. He wishes he could get back to Heartbreak Hotel, but he's lost the directions to Lonely Street. He is finding out that the conquest of inner topology represents difficulties far more complex than crossing an intractable continent in search of fame. He circles the burnt-out car, applying a customary fastidiousness to his awareness of his appearance. He has no intention of spotting his white shoes or purchasing oil on his Kelly green suit. What rises on him is a sense of resolved inner conviction. A voice keeps saying to him, 'Don't give up. You are the chosen one. You are the King.' He has right from the start been impervious to critical disparagement of his stage act. He knows he has it without being able to attribute his dynamic to a source. His two musicians, Scotty Moore and Bill Black, are demeaning him for overadventurous opportunism by the roadside. It's then Marilyn appears again, only he can't tell anyone of this paranormal vision. It's another sighting. She's in white, but she's playing at being dead, with a black aura ringed around her head. She puts a finger to her scarlet lips. A luminous object burns across the clear sky.

Mascara and Gel

Something is rising on the air like a dust storm, a puff of grit, a
confetti of smoking granules in the lazy post-war heat, and the
tension builds to solid momentum, a hand laid flat on the back, and
then a bunched fist impacting the spine. Change loads the air.
Music's the raw current anticipating the breakdown of social values,
a fierce, impulsive marriage of black music and rhythm and blues.
Elvis channels the whole liberated force of the musical directive; the
current burns through his head, hips and genitals. He implodes on
the intensity. He has the plasticity of the protean star, the one who
acts as the prototypical catalyst to change, without even knowing it's
happening.

All those afternoons as a teenager spent window-shopping in
Guy and Bernard Lansky's clothes store on Beale Street, before he
was able to afford his first purchases, were a part of his formative
obsession with clothes. When he acquired his first striped sports jacket
with a velvet collar, and then a black shirt, followed by a pink one,
he was instinctively picking up on the androgyny which was to pre-
occupy the sixties male. Elvis in mascara, his blacked-out eyes
increasing his pansexual appeal to girls writing their names in nail
varnish over his car, the walls of the hotels in which he would stay,
and in imagination in bold red letters over the blue sky. Elvis was set
apart at the beginning of his career by his feminine attention to
minute details of his appearance. He would disappear for hours to
ritualise the combing of his hair.

Changes arrive with a whiphand. Gladys wishes only that he
would quit and buy a furniture store with his first proceeds. But
the storm builds with him in the form of tonic sexual liberation. He is
already a part of an intraspecies. He has to recast himself on stage,
and strike like a snake from the premises of his rebirth. He segues
from Big Joe Turner's 'Shake, Rattle and Roll' to 'Flip, Flop and Fly',
and the uncontrolled energies burn the audience. Men who modify
gender are the leaders of a new future race. Elvis has an almost
kleptomaniacal eye for jewellery at Levitch's in Memphis. 'Nobody's
diamonds will shine like Mr Levitch's,' he is to tell a group of celeb-
rities in Las Vegas. He likes to buy fistfuls of rings and diamonds at a
time. He will then dispense the compact boxes containing diamond-
studded gold jewellery to the people he encounters who show him
little kindnesses.

Elvis meets Jesus Christ in the red Arizona desert, in Hopi country.
Jesus stares at him out of a square pink cloud. The cloud is a lumi-

nously ethereal corolla. He gets out of the tour bus, and stands in a pink denim shirt, arms open to the transparent desert sky. A vulture goes one way, and Jesus the other. Elvis writes a cryptogram in the dust. As they move away, the place breaks into red flowers.

See See Rider

Often it's the black Stutz Blackhawk that Elvis uses to slip out of Graceland at night, accompanied by David and Rick Stanley, his two bodyguards. He's autophobically obsessed with death, and makes periodic visits to the Memphis morgue. Death imageries proliferate in his psyche. He can't let go his fascination with the *puer aeternis*. By identifying so strongly with the fantasy of immutable youth, he is in turn attracted to the complementary descent implied by death. He wants to desomatize consciousness, and live in a state of intermediary reality, without a body. None of his involuntary suicide attempts have reassured him about his status in life or death. When he first attempted to OD in 1967, weeks before his marriage to Priscilla, paramedics had worked to revive him. In his coma, he could hear Vernon shouting, 'Son, please don't die. Don't die.'

In the myth, Psyche has to retrieve her box of beauty from the underworld, presided over by Persephone. In that box is concealed the knowledge of death, but paradoxically she must die in order to know the contents. The King was constantly aware of being in that predicament. To marry the Queen of the underworld, he would have to die, but be unable to report back on his discoveries. In the morgue, the bodies were properly dead; the loved and the anonymous, the successful and the failed. He would bribe the attendants and scrutinize the features of those who had suicided out. He wanted to find a sign, a trace of redemptive certainty in the slack facial muscles of the refrigerated dead. Wouldn't there be a word concealed under somebody's tongue, or beneath an eyelid? Some sort of teleological affirmation that the journey involved a psychological rebirth. His bodyguards pretended not to notice the King's pathologically morbid attraction to corpses. Elvis would wear his messianic white suit for these necrophiliac expeditions. He would pray, act out his ritual as a psychopomp, and then drive back to Graceland at the thrillingly high speed which characterized his driving. Back to cheeseburgers and banana splits, his consolatory engorgements of food, and the ritually spaced three envelopes of cocktailed drugs marked Attack 1, Attack 2, Attack 3. His daily narcotic protocol places him out of bounds of declining record sales and physical dissolution. He can be nearer to Gladys then, for her love is unconditional, and she requires no vindication for his tragic decline. Sometimes, when a
guitar plays itself in the music room, or a wind from nowhere walks through the house, he knows it's her little way of demanding attention. The songs come back, 'Honey Honey', 'Rock-a-Hula Baby', 'My

Way', 'See See Rider'. His sequestration is like disappearance into a black hole. Psyche's box of beauty will be gold encrusted with rhinestones. If he *could* only look inside, he tells himself, he would be the one to survive it. He'll bring the box back to his protective fortress. He strums a guitar, and shambles through a somnambulistic 'See See Rider'.

Real Time

Elvis's days when they involved real time, included mornings, afternoons and nights, spaces he occupied with experiential living. He too stood under a cerulean sky debating on the impossible conundrums of life and death, and walked out to the musically scrolled wrought-iron gates at Graceland, to sign autographs for the assembled faithful. Often he'd ride his hot pink Harley Davidson around the grounds, his fans translating the bike's rubbered noise into the star's erratically zippy trajectory. It was all unreal, whether he was inside or outside. When he asserted himself, through speech, it was often in the form of naturally compounded metaphor. Of Juliet Prowse, with whom he co-starred in *GI Blues*, he said, commenting on her figure, 'She has a body that would make a bishop stamp his foot through a stained-glass window.'

A Capricorn, who owed something of his appearance and legs-apart stance to the comic books character Captain Marvel Jr, from whom he also took the idea of sideburns, and a lock of hair curlicued over the forehead, Elvis seemed psychologically fixated on the idea that he had outlived himself. All the inferior movie roles contracted for him by Colonel Parker had got into his blood as celluloid overload. His record career had been compromised by an affiliation to ersatz Hollywood glamour. He is bored and swallows on it like codeine. He misses the volumeric tension of fans agglomerated into theatre auditoriums, the frenetic buzz of live performance, the lacerating scarification of his clothes, and the idolization which extends to the Russian claim that there is an eight-foot-high statue of the King on Mars. He wants to get off on reality, but he's lost the connection. If he could have the sky airbrushed pink, the trees cobalt and the grass black, then he would participate in the outdoors world. Gladys has always sopped up the natural diversity of the elements.

He tabulates the casualties in his performing world. Eddie Cochran killed in a car accident, and Gene Vincent crippled in the same metallic concertina. Buddy Holly, Ritchie Valens and the Big Bopper all dead in the same plane crash. Jerry Lee Lewis and Chuck Berry both accused of incidents with minors. When Elvis comes in from biking the grounds, he's suddenly shocked into seeing his gold hands under the leather biker's gloves. The glitter spray has remained to transform his hands into royal digits. Inside, an aide drapes an opulent jacket over his shoulders. There are a number of young ingénues waiting to meet him in the mirrored TV room. He forgets they are there, calls for food to be delivered to his bedroom and disappears under the glacial chandeliers at the top of the big stairs. He wants to pray. He wants to conduct a colloquy with the God of benevolence and the God of Placidils. When he prays, he reconnects with his source. The light is bright blue. God is a gospel singer. Elvis can hear him in the back of the sky. He knows now why the gift is on him. There's a summer storm building over Memphis, but the voice continues clear.

Love Me Tender

He likes that song. It reminds him of sarsaparilla milk shakes, and his initial dates with Dixie Locke, riding out to Overton Park, and planting concealed indigo lovebites beneath the shoulder-line of her dress. All the professed fidelities of first love, and the sworn promises to inseparably bonded futures hang in the innocent mellowness of his delivery. Of course the love never comes right, and if it did, the song wouldn't exist with its naïve invocation to a seamlessly united future. It's the absence of the obvious connotative rhyme 'blue' which takes the listener by surprise, given Elvis's lifelong affiliation to real or simulated dejection. It's Elvis's naïvety wins through. If he'd melodramaticized the lyrics, the song would have dropped dead like a stone thrown flatly into a deep pool. As it is the song smells of sarsaparilla and a slow day way down South.

His singular obsession is with fame, and the corresponding alienation it affords. It's his upbringing, and Gladys's insistence on protectively keeping him to herself, which has acclimatized him to inveterate isolation as a star. Elvis knew he was dipping into the blue pool, as soon as girls lacerated the clothes on his body, broke down the dressing-room doors, and had him sit on top of the shower cubicle, while police officers came to his rescue. After that, there's no rehabilitating to reality. His innate sense of inferiority aligns him to the spiritual disclosures of black music, while embodying a white dynamic to orientate the work towards consumerism.

Elvis is deferentially pliable to David Weisbart, who had produced James Dean's *Rebel Without a Cause*, in 1955. *Love Me Tender* is his first Hollywood film, and with Ken Darby accompanying him on piano, he sings the title song, a rewrite of the Civil War ballad 'Aura Lee'. He prefers ballads, although his animalistic stage act rarely allows for the stillness in which to perform pitched songs. Even the film crew are put into abeyance by his perfect rendition of the song. 'I believe that all good things come from God... I don't believe I'd sing the way I do if God hadn't wanted me to. My voice is God's will, not mine,' he told his immediate Hollywood coterie. His manner is always to divert attention from his achievements and attribute them to a higher source on which he's dependent. It's a way of appearing modest in the face of rapidly escalating fame. He works out head arrangements for his songs by having the dub played over and over again. Back at the Beverly Wilshire he has a stepladder sprayed gold and sits on it in order to meditate and eat. He feels the need to be in touch with spirit. Hollywood's like a big diamanté heart on the edge of the sea. He is standing on tiptoe in his blue shoes in the centre of it. The Pacific never stops breathing.

Moody Blue

Sometimes the cocktail of zombifying downers has him sleepwalk through his past at Graceland. Like Marcel Proust, Elvis has interiorized his life to the confines of a bedroom. Day is night and night is day. His insulating red velvet curtains enforce the King's growing sense of time-lessness. He uses polypharmacy – the synergistic reaction of a number of different drugs, Dilaudid, Valium, Meprobamate, Ethchlorvynol, mostly sedative-hypnotic drugs and analgesics. He has two television sets mounted in the ceiling, so that he can watch his favourite pro-grammes without sitting up. His bedroom doors are padded black leather. He wears gold lamé pyjamas, and wonders if he'll ever again know what time it is. His fans have fixed him at a certain point in time, which terminates around his 1973 Aloha from Hawaii globally satellited concert. His iconized image can never change. When he looks at his hair he knows it is white under the black dye. His dysfunc-tional neuroses have centred themselves in the excessive eating of comfort foods, the monolithic portions of pork chops, crisp bacon, cornbread, mashed potatoes and banana puddings on which he has grown to be pendulously adipose. He takes up too much volume in the mirror, there's two of him, three of him, four of him, and he smashes the glass for presenting him with so aberrant a misrepresen-tation of himself.

Elvis's long night stretches to a delusional infinity. He really believes that he'll wake up one day to find himself metamorphosed back to the snake-hipped youthful King. He has had Red West, his long-term bodyguard, take out a murder contract on Priscilla's lover. There's too much time, and there's too little of it. If he runs back down the corri-dor he'll meet a celluloid simulacrum of himself as he was in 1965, and if he runs the other way it's into an unquantified dark in which there may be no one waiting in the big empty room we think of as death. He'd like to believe that his solid gold Cadillac will be garaged for him on the other side. The one finished with forty coats of hand-rubbed glitter paint mixed with crushed diamonds and scintillating fish scales to enhance the sparkle. He had ordered it from Barris Custom City of North Hollywood. He sees the car as connected with his mes-sianic role. It is sent out on tour in his absence, an apocalyptic symbol of the chosen one. His isolation from musicians, screenwriters and directors has always been total. It's as if everything in his career has happened without him. The momentum escalates, while the King retires to his inner court. Today he wants his food dyed the colour of the advance vinyl pressing of 'Moody Blue'. He sits reading in a rhine-stone-emblazoned jacket. The big empty room is also coloured blue, it's like a cobalt auditorium. Gladys is waiting for him there. He's late, but he's also too early.

MEAN AND MOODY

Mean and Moody

Red tie, red socks, he's planned it in advance,
each detail perfect, and the gun polished,
an EP grip-initialled Colt .45,
the chamber loaded, chipped turquoise handle
so companionable to his hand
it warms like a familiar friend
to the impacted pressure that he feeds
unflexing metal. The weapon's a pet
he cradles like something he's tamed
into a complicitous pact.
A rainy Sunday fingerprints the house;
the doo-wop on the stereo
breezes in from another floor. E sniffs
the barrel for its scouring scent
of metal cocktailed with danger,
a crisp inhalation that gets him high
and higher at a second whiff. He'll kill
the impetus to kill himself
with one clean bullet through the brain, erase
the choking pentecostal guilt he feels
at fame won from cool celluloid,
and vinyl pyramided to the sky.
He locks the door, and savours his death-scare,
throws up the gun, and catches it
adroitly, like it's meant to stay
bonded to his weird energies; his dare.
He prods his temple, marks a frontal lobe,
and feels his throat choke dry, his impulse stall
at the cold-terror risk, stands up and shoots
a punch-hole from the hip, a second one
right through a televised gangster
checking his smart fedora in the hall.

All Mussed Up and Prettified

The leopard multiplies collective spots –
an eat-the-heart-out generation's drive
proclaims its romantic ideal,
the singer squeezing lemon on the heart,

it hurts that bad at seventeen
to love a man who outglamours a girl,
her wardrobe flattened by his flash,
his sexuality so taut

its bi-ly dionysian,
peachy with sensual undertow.
The girls are pencil-skirted, bouffanted,
surfing the hip-vocabulary

the singer body-languages as sex.
They're first date kissables, loopy bra straps
vining their arms. Their hero burns a hole
clean through his loafers from impacted beat…

The signal's global like a red love-heart
hologrammed by his pheromones
lit up in every woman's need
to out her sexuality

and top the moment with a strawberry.
The impulse cooks in suburban bedrooms,
hemlines grow shorter, and a red lipstick
called Hound Dog clarifies each mouth's

devotion to its frantic star.
A new dynamic tidal-waves the old,
the girls keep shaping bit by bit
a genderless heart-throb fetish,

the sexes interfacing, girlie push
bringing the singer to his knees
in face to shoe acknowledgement
his stove pants hurt along the straining seam.

Private Presley in Paris

The boredom grips like ice around his boots,
a GI's Friedberg winter, bluesy lows,
impacted freeze, the peanut butter thin,
no grained impasto texture on a wedge…

His battle-ready excellence grows slick,
an Operation Snowman raid at dawn.
He outs for Paris, showcasing the gang,
the night train lit with a peach-glow in first,

the darkness hitting by like speeded film.
A phallocratic party. What they'll win
is girls in excess, orgiastic romp,
red-suited in the Hôtel Prince de Galles,

the chandelier-blaze slung like glacial jewels
rainbowing Louis XVI furniture.
They drive towards a city overview,
late night, and watch a rose and orange dawn

blast auroral eruptions on white cold.
He writes the memory into his heart
as though he brought a blood orange
alive that moment in his hand…

Fishnetted chorines ruck his satin sheets,
girls lifted from the Lido, Le Bantu,
they pour into his need, a chocolate box
landslides in tumbling nuggets to the floor.

Elvis sings 'I'll be Home Again' to June,
her puckered lipstick pouts blotch on his neck,
their distribution like a rain-smashed flower.
The city stretches bridge by bridge at dawn.

Out window-shopping, he throws back his head
in funky amazement as French girls run
shoeless to meet him in the glaze, a blonde
smudging her tears before she starts to scream.

Moulin Rouge, Munich (1959)

Her tongue's like a liana
in his mouth, a tricky lexicon
of sensual keyboarding.
Her fingers kerb-crawl at his waist.
She's leggy Nina, redoing
ambitions graded in his brain,
enticing him to run away
with her, he'll reidentify,
reclusive by an Alpine lake
depth-blue as lapis lazuli,
she minky, diamonded,
exclusive inamorata
detaining him from hobbyist
fanatics, mystiqueing his fame.
The champagne sugars racily;
she kicks her shoes off, lacquered toes
a gestural vocabulary.
They'll leave at dawn, despite the snow
oceloting each throughish train.
His head bangs with the fantasy –
the big escape, the left-behinds,
the headlined global elegy
at intimations of his suicide
or break for anonymity.
Nina positions on his lap
entreating that it's all for real,
a once and only love
bitten into their veins, a soup
chemistried for two.
Elvis is seeing chandeliers
each time her fingerpads website
a tormentable nerve.
She sucks a cherry from his glass;
Nina's the sunrise and the tops,
rolling the red globe on his lips,
twisting it round, making a gap
until it drops.

Fatigues and Manoeuvres

Buffed duffel bag, stylized military hat,
Elvis bashes weird military,
a heart-throb conscript inspiring recruits,
he yawns plush plaid-blanketed, pink cat's ears
triangled for the million-dollar deal

for which he'll field the telephone
on USS *General Randall*.
The ship retrieves itself in push-up swell,
a muscled rise and fall green sea
slugging obdurate metal,

having him lurch on swimmer's legs
to scoop the call.
At night his mother moonwalks through his dreams,
she's broken her glass coffin lid
and diamond shards stick in her blue nightie.

Elvis is spit-shine macho to his squad,
his roommate Charlie Hodge oodles guitar
virtuoso, and keeps him sane.
They're headed to Grafenwöhr. Private E
anecdotes Hollywood: déclassée blondes.

In Bad Nauheim, his fridge is overstocked.
The girls are a teeny plurality
of redhead kittens in his bed.
He flat-out attacks every menial task,
sanding a jeep's rust freckles to clean lick.

Once, in a jeep, snowed under for the night,
the engine leaking carbon monoxide
he blacked out, got cuffed back by air
and crawled outside into blue snow,
his DNA code typed into the stars...

Hand-tailored khakis, purple hearts,
Elvis sleepwalked through nightmares trailing sheets
like bridal gowns, and next day showed his best,
screeching a white BMW into base
and exiting in one stripe green fatigues.

Hairsprays and Crooning

Serendipitous vinyl cache
stashed on his Goethestrasse floors,
Elvis's crooner library
has debonair-imaged sleeves,
velvety-larynxed Dean Martin,
Vic Damone and Jackie Wilson,
Sinatra's bel canto diary
of lowlight Big Apple betrayals,
Sam Cooke's grainier timbre,
Mel Tormé's blue-mood reveries,
Bennett's Latinate fluency,
Johnnie Ray's quavery vibrato
and the histrionically purple
Mario Lanza,
                O Sole Mio
played over and over
as a vocal tutorial,
a diaphragmatic tattoo
retrieved as 'It's Now or Never'.

Elvis's two-and-a-half-octave range
has his baritone nail high G's
and A's in rotund voice.
He's the ascendant maestro
pitched into world-reform,
his bumped quiff like hairsprayed liquorice,
his concentration dead on.
His breath-control index measures
ten paces with inhalation
before the expulsion's punched.
Fans gather outside for tone,
as Elvis tactics the changes,
dramatizes delivery
to an other-sided audience,
rolls up his shirt sleeves and pitches
an a cappella O Sole Mio,
the phrasing perfect as any
unrehearsed domestic demo.

Elvis Blackmailed

Bare-torsoed, flaunty
in black shorts,
Elvis is spine-orchestrated,
youth-gelled and bio-organized,
face down, then face up
on a pre-prepared purple couch,

the dermatologist's fingers
creating a tabla rasa
on tendrily wrinkles.
Carnation, mimosa, rosewood
are note-specific aroma
sandalwood dubbed on to bass-lines.

Elvis submits to undulant
mapping across his features,
treats Landau as confessor
about Priscilla Beaulieu
unconsciously feeds his kinkies
on to collecting tape.

Aroma cocktails his skin
he'd like to look like Liz Taylor,
every decade he's promised
he'll be twenty years younger,
rhinoplasty will follow
his seamless epidermis.

Landau's fingerprints snare-drum
from pectorals to balls,
shocking guitar-shaped Elvis
into a threatening posture
loud with recriminations
later with denial.

Therapy's discontinued,
Elvis sulks like a sack,
both men retract their repertoire
of knowing on the other,
both need disinformation
complicitous in that pact.

Elvis kills his short-fuse temper,
shovels dollars for the tapes,
unpacks wads from a valise,
a nerve below his waist
left to go out like a light bulb
in the cavernous Berlin hall.

Catching Kisses on a Drop-dead Day

Priscilla's windowed by a babydoll,
a transparent pink statement to the hips.
Her eyelashes are Maybelline daisies,

grainy twistings from a mascara brush.
Elvis has gone trout fishing for rainbows,
his green suit dips like spring into the lake,

a liquefied, flashy, bulked emerald.
He sits on a bruised Bible. Zippy flies
do gaudy splash-downs on the tricked surface.

The girls are sunning in string bikinis,
and Elvised by his miraculous hex
place kisses on his neck like strawberries,

repart and restructure his collapsed hair.
The guys keep banging up the stereo
on flimsy pop. Girlie groups pink the wide

uncensored air sheeting above water.
They're miles form home, and miles from anywhere;
a trout jumps nose-up for a turquoise bug.

Elvis gets smoochy with a green-eyed one,
whose 36D cups nudge at his chin.
His detached sweet talk sounds overrehearsed,

his manners are like velvet to her ear.
Priscilla's bored with waiting, and the house
refrigerates kitsch right to its chandeliers.

Teeny Polaroids

I

She's babydolled in every pastel shade,
and keeps a handgun in her underwear.
He isolates her so she'll never fade.

II

She's sixteen, fêted by his epic stance,
reverence for piscine virginity.
His come on is a corybantic dance.

III

She banshees down the central scarlet stair,
white blouse, plaid skirt and overtakes herself
presenting squid-ink noodles as her hair.

IV

His voyeuristically asexual fad
has her position as peek geometry.
The shutter absolves him from being bad.

V

She's sassily demure, and sucks a thumb,
eyes looking from their corners, splayed legs arched,
he likes his ingénue to pose dumb.

VI

He goes for Polaroid immediacy,
white cotton panties, Lolita-ish tease,
the pubis an off-limits fantasy.

VII

Hermetically roomed into photo-sex,
he paints her toenails red. Her vaulted legs
are the proscenium to a vortex.

VIII

They costume change in bizarre repertoire,
he shoots a video as she cavorts
in tumbling somersaults across the floor.

Black Coffee

Black Blue Mountain
ground and percolated
pitch,

muddy as the Mississippi
aromatic
as a memory-sachet

split open on shampoo.
Elvis lifts off to head-kicks
the depth-brew bites that hard

in neural weaponry.
Caffeine tracks through his cells
as adrenalized info,

an Aztec god of flash
going central.
To him it's like a river

hurrying with shock.
It means sensory clearance,
a window on the day

foggy dispersals.
He likes his blend obsidian,
overkilled with tang.

Mostly the drink's cavernous
as though he corridored
a march to the interior

and stood over a pool
sunk there for the ritual
and dived right in,

spiralled back revivified,
surer now the bitter
froth sat on his lip.

Wall of Love

A magic-markered love-heart bleeds a name
scored in with passion, crude, ingenuous
want as it registers in someone's life

inked on the boundary wall's graffiti map
of lipsticked declarations. 'Eat my heart
like a blood orange', 'Kill me in your arms

and Love Me Tender in Eternity'
are standouts in the daily love letter
dictated to the King: a diagrammed

collective, written from an open vein…
Elvis reviews the gates each day at five,
his gold palomino's fireballish gloss

autumned in late light crawls with buggish flies.
His buckskin boots are cradled at its sides,
the horse brings nothing but a primal wall

to seeing, refutes everything that's new.
Elvis sips at the glitter in his life,
like iridescent detail that won't stay,

and scans the impromptu vocabulary
as though a species from another star
collectivized a freaky in-the-face

infatuation with him on the hill,
wrote up their messages, and went away,
leaving the mansion time-warped under trees.

Every Girl in the World

My cut-out pin-up posters every wall,
a kiss-curl comma black as melting tar
mapped on my forehead. I'm contagious, hot,
a mean cat arrowed to a bleeding heart,

the sacrificial hound dog running hard
out of the South to royal it on a throne
galaxied with rhinestoned-glitter excess,
my image fed on by a sisterhood

of bleeding Revlon and Max Factor pouts.
The iconized country-boy balladeer,
I got a counterpane of black panties
sewn like an undulant snake on my back...

Women, they fall like roses blown apart,
I couldn't move for jostled laissez-faire,
the feline, like Priscilla, and the rest
atomized into stardust on my lips,

all of them, facets of my mother's love,
devotional prompters of my chart success,
the red-haired, black-haired, blonde, or russet ones,
girls scooping up the dust on which I'd walked

in blue suede shoes: or lying on my car.
I'm targeted, an effigial dude
fantasized over, bitten on my neck,
the one materialized from record sleeves

as Mr Blue Mood, circa 1958,
the eat-your-heart-out, doe-eyed archetype,
making it big as dionysian
provocateur; innocent, impudent,

down on my knees, and flexing like a whip
to riotous pudenda, one and all,
Me out cold, backstage, bigger than the wind
breezing up skirts along the boulevard.

A Day Away From Being Elvis

He screens the limo in the Memphis hills,
and collects lungfuls of post-summer haze,
a head frisked by upgraded air.
She's waiting for him, sketchbook on her knee,
the still-point to a fugitive affair,
her pencil tasselling an oak's
dependably mean-rooted drive
to earth for fluent centuries in one spot.
She's booted, bare-midriffed, blue-jeaned
and ambienced by Chanel riffs.
She's Rita, and his double ee
dispenses with the breezy i.
She chiaroscuroes light and shade and talks
in Elvis fantasy. They live
in re-created Graceland in the woods
and have a cat called Cinnamon
with painted nails. One month each year
Elvis will bust reclusion for Vegas,
the King of Rhinestones colouring his songs
with shot-gold glory.
                        Now they pat the breeze
like an arriving handball, kill the day
by substituting fantasy.
He'll marry Rita by the rising sun
inside the outline of a star,
the minister a born-again alien
fitting a strawberry-sized diamond
to Rita's finger, while the groom
strums a guitar in a high tree.
They'll live with animals, and formulate
a private language, like dipping their words
in strawberry ice cream as emollient.
Their children will be Martian-wannabes,
programmed with netlink access to the stars.

They talk, and Elvis lazes out of time.
When she rolls over, she's so kittenish
a breath excites her, and their dreams pick up
a body rhythm, like increase of rain
brilliantly spent from a mauve thundercloud.

THE SIXTIES: CHARLIE MANSON'S IN THE HILLS

Dead Elvis (1961–69)

Boredom's the trout too slow to clip the fly's
holographic insignia,
its water-skier's shimmer left untouched

on ticking silk. Elvis suffers brain-fade,
twenty-one formulaic films
have toxed his nerves, defused the power lines

by which he handled a mike like a snake.
Robotic, latex-skinned, and furred from junk,
he swallows on a wooden-hearted script,

no guava juice in the block-bite
of frazzled text. The words moonwalk, then drop.
They plug his thinking with barbiturate.

Elvis is property; he's celluloid.
He lives as virtual image, no one there,
his empty Cadillac sent out on tour

as a gold funeral car. He spoons his pie
and drives a beaten panel truck
for anonymity on the bashed roads

he worked as a pre-star itinerary.
Money and cholesterol sew up his veins.
His tantrums shoot to kill: he breaks a chair

to hear a rigid structure give
against the grain. Hollywood's a black dress
he slashes open on a mannequin.

The Sixties

A tidal wave slams thunder on the beach,
the violent uproar in its undertow
communicated as shock frequencies
to bikers sitting out along the road…

Changes dance in a marijuana haze,
an acrid weed-fog feeds defiant youth.
They come together on a loaded vine
at Woodstock, Monterey, the Isle of Wight,

all beads and boots, the men dressed Regency,
his shirt surfing with frill-stacked lace,
her mini, a pink satin afterthought
to being naked. Now it's 'Purple Haze'

freak-storms the airwaves with its driving riffs;
the drugs turn visionary, a microdot
activates all the glowering archetypes.
Lee Harvey Oswald sights a temple vein

big as a power line and blows Kennedy
into death's silent auditorium.
Everywhere insurrection. Monroe dead,
her blonde hair blowing through infinity…

The King stays underground, shored up on pills
to numb his isolation, clouded fame.
He sleeps all day. His rivals strut the boards
windstormed by overloaded decibels,

an insolently hip Mick Jagger preens
into a sea of lookalikes, one hand
controlling thirty thousand devotees.
Somebody high on acid, starts to pray…

Elvis retreats into his king-size bed,
resentful of a marriage he would smash.
Priscilla blue-rooms mornings on her own,
the fuse-blown decade building to its crash.

Hollywood Highs

They're mostly aura-free, diamond-hearted
ensconced glitterati – hyper-real stars
mind-sculpted into celluloid.
Two stuffed leopards crouch by a heart-shaped pool,
a third's positioned on the diving board's
mink trim. Callas weighs in the speaker stacks

stepping in and out of registers
like costume changes. Pool cocktails
are garnished with a short-stemmed flower.
The drag act wears a chandelier earring

clipped to a leopardspot G-string,
body spraypainted with silver daisies.
The woman could be Jane Fonda
handbagging a cosmetic counterload
to tube out a gold mascara.

Nobody's real-timed in dystopia.
Pool filters drone, radio trafficopters
insect a gridlocked traffic queue.
The sky's another B-movie, too long

and storyless to occupy.
Another mansion on, a blonde marries
her lover's murdered body, blood-kisses
the bullet hole for ceremonials,
watched over by the masked killer.

Elvis keeps photophobically inside,
avoids the topless partyers,
sex dwarves and caviar rapacious cats
in purple neon necklaces,
speaks Memphis to his gang, stays cool that way
in chill-out reclusion, his Bel Air space
raw with his crudely untamed energies.

Bel Air Mansions

Elvis leaves snakeskin loafers in the hall;
a hatted Cyclops with a pear-shaped base
professes to a speckled lollipop

his weird obsession to keep buying lamps
as though they're sculptural confectionary,
quasi art-deco fixtures, hardware spoofs

cluttering in mauve turbans, pink flowerpots.
He's a zoo-keeper to compulsive hits
of purchase on the road to Hollywood,

but mostly lamps, the kitschy, tasselled kind
to be transported back home, where the South
hides its indigenous face beneath oaks,

and Gladys sits bug-frazzled on the porch,
nipping at bourbon. Elvis lives by night,
a jukebox, pool table, racing car track

circuited on the boot-shy pile. The girls
are proto-groupies, gobsmack Cupid's bows,
mascara brushed to blue caterpillars,

cat people rounded up for the King cat.
Elvis is bilocated, fly-by-night;
diffident and unflexing, sneeringly

off-limits to the blue-rocked, stardust set.
His cars all point to Memphis: polished hoods
and buffed chrome sleeky panthered in the drive.

Death Valley

Ape-hanger choppers frying in the heat;
a biker's throttled reverb blasts
a sonic apocalypse in the noon.
The mountains squat like yogis in blue haze.

Back of a grizzled lean-to's blaze
Manson death-trips on LSD.
He thinks he's Rommel to the Family,
a desert prophet heeled by naked slaves.

Presley's on the agenda. Sharon Tate
awaits a sacrificial kill.
Charlie can see it all. The sealed mansion
torched by his leather orgiasts.

His head buzzes with 'Eight Miles High',
the Byrds lilting ethereality
suggesting timelessness, a dream-summer
lit by a purple, psychedelic sun.

A drug-fazed girl ivied by hippie beads
listens to Charlie free-associate
prophetic stuff. He tells her death is life;
the victim thanks the killer for his gun.

A wedge of stolen cars arrest the glare.
The girl's occulted by her leader's pull;
she stitches someone's jeans with scarlet thread;
her child is microdotted into space.

Tonight there'll be a raid. Search and Destroy
is logoed on each biker's death's-head back.
Charlie intones a mantra, reads the sky,
and quizzically dissects a broken toy.

Larry Geller's Pink Interlude

Elvis's black hair's like a mandarin's,
gossamer-textured, dyed cobalt,
fluent with Larry's figurative line –

the King's locks counted out like gold
lifted from root capillaries.
Larry's the guru, suspect gay
Bel Air infiltrator, meridianed
by touch to his rich client's spine.

Stylist with Jay Sebring Beverly Hills,
he idolizes glitzy stars.
His cashmere jumper's dusky pink,
a Guerlain high note trips out of a sleeve…

He counsels Elvis in the onion-twist,
you strip the layers to reach the core.
It's self-realization that's truth,
and Yogi Paramahansa reveals
the inner space in which to sit

cushioned by a cloud's levity.
Elvis drops acid, and the fan-tailed fish
blipping in his aquarium
striptease their tropical membranes,

implode, explode as meteors.
The carpet pours into a waterfall.
He thinks the clouds move at his breath,
an exhalation and they stream across

in pyramidal continuity.
Larry's on hand, and Elvis reads the light,
deepens all summer, god-searches
his meditative mind-set, knows he'll die
from overreach, but keeps it near,

a trust that opens like a flower
turned to the source, a blue morning glory
coloured the blue of the Pacific sky.

Presley's Powder-puff Pals

Elvis keeps stage made-up indoors,
severe in black, he's contemporary myth
loafing in the New Washington Hotel,
penthoused like a rare beetle exhibit,
so cut off he's like a soluble pill

ticking to fizzed conclusion in a glass.
He lives for partytime; his court
is jestered by a chimpanzee
dashy in a red velvet coat,
snowballing grungy scatter at the walls…

Nobody knows Elvis's teen secret
kept under Graceland wraps, the doll
pharaohed amongst glitzy heirlooms –
Priscilla who opens doors in his heart,
and stays there, locked inside without a key.

The Memphis gang improvise slaphappy
combatant mashed potato fights
at table, or glutinous dessert crowns,
banana tiara treacling the hair,
the twelve disciples surrealized by goo.

The girls are conventional seraglio,
star-struck, mini-skirted, festy groupies
blocked round the soft glow TV maxi-screen,
a cable apotheosis
Elvis presides over with rawburst quips,

impromptu up there bandit parts.
A jar of amyl nitrate's on the floor.
The girls do mascara. The gang inspect
their stockinged feet, for E's small preference,
his pedic obsession with Chinese shrink.

Their all-nighters are themed by fun,
Elvis's raison d'être, impulsed credo
to cram the moment, find the comic note
in everything – 'You only die once, Jack,
there's no return for a spotlit encore.'

Dressing Marilyn Monroe

The line should never disagree
or adopt its own tangent. It's her curves
create the dress, give shape to gold lamé,
the flesh-coloured buttons sewn into her net bra
accentuate the nipples. It's a trick
adopted from Marlene Dietrich,
breasts pushed up
in a deep V'd halterneck, or she's stitched
into a skirt constrictive as clingfilm,
not even a suspender strap
smudging the contour, despite two black seams
verticalized from Cuban heels.
The aesthetic's to sheathe her nude
fully dressed on spike heels, and entertain
the notion of her leading up high stairs
to a Chanel-soapy boudoir,
her powder granules dusting black silk sheets…

Mostly she's an illusion. We impose
the image we expect, the contoured dress,
one knee angled forward, hands on the hips,
the dumb showgirl's glossy pucker,
or think of her making up, dark lipstick,
tinctures of spicy Shalimar,
hair in a towel, nothing but silk panties
on her tanned body and the swimming pool
outside the window open like a rose.

JFK's Got a New Blue Suit

Marilyn's poured across the presidential desk,
bra-popping in a sewn-on gown,
atomized Shalimar percolating
a spicy high note from dubbed undertones,
a scent frisson with Jackie's staid Chanel.
Fortified by frosted Dom Pérignon,
the President's steel crisis loses grip,
its red-alert taut nerves relax,
as Marilyn tweaks a collar button
and tendrils a cajoling fingernail
across his buttressed lip.
                                   Her showing slip
is like a black lace watermark.
Neither are osmotic to Presley's glam,
they trivialize the androgyne
as hair bleach the decade will wash away.
He's self-commodified, irreverent,
generation-specific, and her mouth
goes strawberry on shaping J's
into an oval. Her left hand frog-walks
to lift a steno pad for its number,
a rival's coded numerals.
The fizz rainstorms across her tongue
tasting of sunny nostalgia.
She's used, and desperate to his presenting face
or is it Bobby's? as he pulls away
suspicious of her coaxing sobriquets…
He's dilemmaed, not fielding calls,
the paranoia in him sizing up
like an inflatable doll. Now she slaps
him upper right, and sees a wrinkle twitch,

exits in a spectacular,
a heel snapping at her indignant stomp,
and outside, hears a speakered 'Jailhouse Rock'
demands attention for assault,
burns on a slow-fuse temper, swings around,
and sashays laughing into the mad street.

Baritone Marilyn Monroe

She's divaesque scandal
druggy bimbo dripping sequins
the archetypal bottle-blonde
chocolate Cuban heel and toepiece
peeping through a strappy sandal

Bimboed by the Kennedys
in a nude designer gown
Elvis meets comparison
in his festy paste-jewelled jumpsuits
posturing as sleaze striptease

Iconized, legendized,
36-22-33
Marilyn's vampy spangles seem
provocation in a zip
intelligence unrealized

all spaghetti straps and seams,
gluteal choreography
worked over for surface appeal
Marilyn and Elvis dare
plug in to designer dreams

She's used up by narcotic nights
downers and neat Sapphire gin
he metabolizes fame
as chemical toxicity
she's beaten black and blue in fights

Both are reverentially
encouraged to generate
self-immolate, déclassé zones
living out expectations
for the twentieth century

Elvis's Secret Psychedelic Recordings (1965)

Cool Blue Trip

A fuzzbox riff secretly LA canned.
The lyrics have a gold-tailed black rainbow
shimmer to kaftan gurus up on trip.

Pink Elephant's Graveyard

The cemetery's blonde watchman's Jayne Mansfield.
The outtake glitches where a nuked pink car
jumps barriers right into an open grave.

Candy's Pink Vision

A jazzy inflection rains funk-rock grooves.
Candy flits mushroom-spotting through wet woods.
A pink hare hands her his pink ballet shoes.

Elise's Acid Tears

The double-stacked Marshalls thunder reverb.
Over wah-wah insistence Elvis sings
of blue tears dissolving a mountainside.

I'm Thinking High

A Hendrix copy jams. The song's up high.
He sings of love as karmic LSD.
His woman's dressed in purple in the sky.

U Spot UFOs

Sitars, then harped ethereality.
The voice delay is ceilinged in the stars
and sings of saucers blipping through blue space.

Marriage

His mind's fidgety like a spider's legs.
Laired in his bedroom sipping liberty,
he won't come out, despite the waiting car's
idle remonstrance, tyre wall grips
pleated in gravel like stitchwork. He broods

black thunderclouds inside his sanctuary.
He fears the retributive law,
the teen girl he preserved in rich honey,
his female Elvis, mirror counterpart
picking the stitches out of his gold shirt…

His aunt dusts knuckles on the pearl-glass paint.
He hangs in his interior,
black-suited, wrinkling a silk tux,
defiance crumbling under pressured threat,
but nurturing the moments like his last

on earth: awkward defiance in his eyes
at going public. When he pulls downstairs
stored hatred of the Colonel has him stamp.
His bride's a simulacrum fantasy,
an off-the-rack tulle gown. No one there.

A Las Vegas wedding, the red suite's flushed
with patisserie flowers, the six-tiered cake's
a spun-sugar high-rise, candied volutes
there for the earthquake crack, the pointing knife
toppling a virgin deck with one clean cut…

He surfs the flash guns. She's Egyptian-eyed.
They'll Learjet out, but for a time he's dead
to everything, but how resentment builds
inside him to a still black reservoir
waiting to rip barriers and tear free.

'68 Comeback Special

The panic shock-waves backstage, freaks a storm
in his adrenalin. At thirty-three
he's real-time obsolete, ex-celluloid.
His make-up runs in inky rivulets

and is corrected. He is sweat-glazed shakes,
black leather Kamikaze candidate
stood at the entrance to a dark hallway
awaiting his transition to the lights,

the studio's explosively live capsule.
Cued-on he's body-lit by orange spots,
misreads the lyrics, and Heartbreak Hotel
is gappy, dry-throated, presenced by fear,

a faltering, human Lonely Street, then eased
he curls a lip, rakes one hand in the air
and bleeds into 'Can't Help Falling in Love',
eerie vibrato catching at the heart...

He wakes suddenly in a new decade,
the time warp wiped, as though back from the dead
his jump-start reincarnation adopts
residual aura with a pop cat's sleek

attention-grabbing mystique. Now he preens
his voice on 'Love Me Tender', sings direct
into the bleachers; he's the first and last
lifting the orange peel on sentiment

to have a generation repossess
unashamed rites of love. It's in his tone,
inheritance as change – his downward look
begs he's remembered always as he shifts

to right brain dominance, takes the hand-mike
and feels himself expand, he's in the song
so totally, he's global with his breath
posting a love-heart to the universe.

Black Leather Skins

Worn for the day, as macho-specific,
they're a slick-sheened godskin, oilily black
as garage floor spillovers

staining obsidian.
Rain-glow pigmented, they're youth-hide
made to look lived in
before outed on stage

as a Hollywood eye-stopper
a '68 day of creation
ripply spellbinder,
a once only absolute
cut from anonymous herds.

Elvis's are rebel-tone black
like a biker's epidermis.
He's a dionysian panther

suppressing a histrionic
pitch for vocal rotunda,
notes open like amaryllis
voice-brushed by Maria Callas…

He's the displaced Snake King's
ophidian reincarnation,
the swankily sassy liberal-spender,

head-bowed, quixotically shamming,
reading his notes like blue shade
as he slows to 'Love Me Tender'.

Circle G Ranch

Pilled mania in the blowily white cold,
a mauve sky fluffing low over Horn Lake,
his eyes throw wonder through sheer clarity
of seeing diamonded on the skyline

a shine-out antebellum plantation house
so there it doesn't seem to stay,
a twenty-foot-high concrete cross begging
the owner be a sacrificial god…

It's his in four days. Blue snow pacts with ice.
He paces boundaries, breath signing the air
as vaporous calligraphy,
snowballing dazzle at a moon-faced wall,

bored by midday, then sullen by the fire.
A green garbage sack filled with hot dog buns
humped by his side, he trailers with the gang,
a hip prospector in bucolic sham,

collecting Rancheros, Deluxe Chevys,
gridlocked metal that burns beneath the foot…
The ranch chews money like a bitten tape
looping to digital inconsequence.

Priscilla's love nest's bootmarked by the guys,
Elvis's in-house macho camaraderie
winning the precinct with their one-liners,
a citified coterie tractoring

acres that crowd on to vanishing point.
Priscilla's us and them, cuts at an edge,
hysterically deposed, she shares the lot,
cooks for all twelve, then blows back to Memphis,

while Elvis counts his losses, ruins crops,
rides his gold horse towards the setting sun
in a mock shoot-out, has the boys scatter
and drop down dead, arms raised to say he's won.

CONTEMPORARIES

John Lennon

Arriving out of nowhere. Retrospect
reads revolution into accident,
somebody breaking into a decade
to invent the sixties, stand on its head

post-war inertia. The black knitted tie,
fringe to the eyebrows, stack-heeled boots replaced
by kaftans, Indian beads, an acid trip
standing a forest in the sky;
a little girl rides on an elephant
out of her dream into another dream.
The universe fits neatly in his eye.

Banging a piano in an empty room,
New York outside, it all happened too fast.
He searches for a melody
to clarify the changes. He's withdrawn
into another vision, white on white
or black on black, both are the same
keys to invisibility.
The songs are messages, and they return
to we who listen as the sunlight falls
over the late part of a century,
deciding what is gone and what will last.

Jimi Hendrix

The fuzzbox virtuoso
cherokee. His blues voice talks to his guitar's
distorted eloquence, there's nothing he
can't afford an improvised melody,
hair tied back by a scarlet bandanna,
his chords so individually

his own, they characterize the sixties.
Take a flamboyant cocktail of mixed drugs
and run naked into a turquoise sea
and that's a JH song. A mauve starfish

opens to reveal an interior
in which an underwater city shows.
Small fish swim in and out of someone's eyes.
He keeps the vision. Later, it is wild,
his punishing, phallic solo,

his using the guitar to emphasize
a sexual geometry, building a storm
around him, a circular hurricane,
the sort that picks a house up like a toy

then drops it in a tidal wave.
He's tuned to something deep black as the night
which tears him out of life, attenuates
his earthing, pulls the switch on him,
fuses the mains which read House Lights.

Jim Morrison

Somebody always has to disappear,
and so the myth travels the way a seed
blazes into a red poppy
beside the road. Tatters of wind-nagged silk.

The voice can't change now. It is posthumous;
a sixties product. I can hear it scream
out of a wind tunnel, an underpass,
it seems to issue from a blue-black dream

in which the figure standing at the bar
turns round to find the world has disappeared,
he stands on the edge of a precipice,
nothing behind him but the radial star

his whisky tumbler smashed in the mirror.
The bottles are all empty. Jack Daniel's,
White Label, Jim Beam, a drained Cutty Sark.
The bartender walks straight out through the dark

and floats to nowhere. Unshaven, obese,
Jim looks for handholds. If he tries to sit
on the stained counter he'll have vertigo.
What he misses is the microphone stand,

getting off on stage, fast adrenalin.
Is this Paris or LA? Night or day?
He suffers from a drugged amnesia.
A blue snake winds itself around his hand.

He'll stay here, drinking like Malcolm Lowry,
until his vision clarifies. Out there,
a red mountain pushes for a gold sky.
He'll climb there later to meet a black bear.

Brian Jones

So delicate an intrusion on noise,
a sitar, harpsichord, peacock's feather,
always the right tone in the melody,
a slide-guitar or dulcimer, blond hair
shielding the eyes, no gender clue

offered in the lace blouse, mandarin coat,
jewellery picked up from Saks Fifth Avenue,
velvets from the Chelsea Antique Market.
Rejected, one way through is to mutate

to a new species, go away from life
and reinvent it, become solitary,
the only one looking out for others.
In time, the mutants, trans-people arrive
and infiltrate at festivals.
They are the enlightened ones, dressed in gold,

they live behind the hills or else nowhere.
It's a story of degeneration,
how drink and drugs get into overdrive
and how the fingers no longer find chords,

but tremble. It's the myth of dying young
recurs as a brutal reality.
Brian Jones face down in his swimming pool
murdered one sultry July night,
a ritual sacrifice to the sixties.

Four Decades of Jagger

And that's too little for uncompromise,
raising a whiphand to conformity;
the skinny, unkempt schoolboy in hipsters,
mean with maracas, pulling a surprise

on the establishment's dead machismo,
daring to make a fashion of long hair,
high-heeled boots, pouting so the Negroid lips
made the wide ovoid of fellatio

around a phallic microphone. And live,
so dynamized, an electric dervish
slowing to a falsetto blues; few thought
your hyped-up extroversion would survive

more than a year or two; but you had air,
that unnamed particle which once released
is self-expansive, power that blows through walls,
its hard pressure pinpointed in your stare

that goes on holding crowds in abeyance;
now it is mega-stadiums, hard rock,
and you're still energized, youthful, a slap
to the disclaimers who you will outdance

a lifetime. You're from Egon Schiele's art,
one hand on the hip, a contortionist's
agility – prototypal rebel,
we think no love-arrow could pierce your heart

because you're everyone's. And what you've made
from public confrontation is a role
that liberates and grows to a statement
about ourselves; how we are less afraid

to be the individual. Look, you say,
the age grows with us: the music is tight
and graduates, the vocals pitched up high.
The town is closed because you're on today.

The Rolling Stones

An unrestrainable storm's energy,
a blues tornado building year by year,
smashing successive decades like stage props
into a singular reality –

the music's drive, and how Keith Richards loads
that power line with such a laid-back style
he might be anywhere the drug dictates;
and now in high key the dervish explodes

frenetically, adopting a persona
for each volatile lyric expression,
a manically improvised Lucifer,
a lashingly exploitative 'Gimme Shelter',

a transsexual identity which dares
contain a crowd that's like an exodus
come across country for the new ideal,
and with the red light on, it really scares,

Jagger's psychopathic 'Midnight Rambler',
cued up to stick a knife right through the throat,
a pyrotechnical 'Jumpin' Jack Flash',
no ostentation from the bass player,

it's all up front by a shared microphone,
and what was revolutionary is still
an ongoing assessment of our lives,
survival, altered consciousness, a tone

that challenges the way we live and think,
and devastates the old world, moves into
the centre of new chaos, while the pack
flail for the singer on the spotlit brink...

Keith Richards

So laid back, living where his dimension
touches on inner vision, that far gone
he wouldn't notice a black spotting fly
settle on a cheek and a second one

glint as a double beauty mark.
Heroin as an embalming fluid,
a cellular rejuvenator, he's
like Burroughs, a human experiment

in survival. Fortified, whisky-shot,
the music lines are always tight, the nerves
feel into that non-committal control;
the man lives for the chords he generates,

and is a kind of latter-day Crowley,
an adept of a deathless state, someone
who guards somatic knowledge, most alive
confronting stadia; knee boots, jewellery,

fetishistic tinctures of Joy,
hair brushed in every way that's contrary,
the archetypal rock star, maintaining
the image as reality

through so many mutations, Swiss clinics,
and in retreat at Redlands, someone who
finds a centre in the crazy decades.
'I'm dying, but that means I'm living too'.

Marc Bolan

So diminutive even up on heels,
his eyes are two black craters; he commits
the lyric to an understated drawl,
a moody venom injected with hints

that it's not all an act, and the guitar
pursues descending phrases, solo licks
that vitalize a time peculiar
to his predominance, a glam guru

statuette-sized as Wagner or Lautrec
in a rainstorm of sequins. He is mean
in ways the audience demand,
untouchable, withdrawn beneath rucked hair,

a style, a genre without a precedent,
and soon used up, burnt-out current,
no visible transition, one foot snared
in past successes, one without a hold

on shifting, earthquake ground, a silver boot…
The myth's to die incomplete, unfulfilled,
and sometimes it proves a reality,
a miscalculation behind the wheel,

the car's tin can concertina,
all aspirations left illusory,
uncontactable, sirens everywhere,
a crow taking off to a nearby tree.

David Bowie

Today the streetwise emulate
things you abandoned years ago –
pantomorphic chameleon
changing colours like the gecko

from Ziggy's sequined leotards
to Berlin's stark cabaret clothes,
cradling your death wish in a skull
before letting the whole act go –

setting the tone for the austere
soundless grey wave that broke over
an age drifting like a canoe
to the lip of a whirlpool;

the blue cinematic cut-ups of Low.
Post-futuristic, you pointed
a way forward every three years,
outstripping your discoveries

like a child the ingenious kites
he's flown once for the aerial high,
the baling out of an umbilical
constraining a scarlet stingray.

We think of you confronting a mirror,
contriving new facial geometries,
one green eye, one eye blue, with Picasso's
genius to find asymmetry

in angles and planes of a face.
The new mix will be pyrotechnical,
the sounding into zero – Major Tom's
cremated ashes buried in deep space.

FIVE FAN LETTERS
TO JESUS CHRIST

Five Fan Letters from Elvis to Jesus Christ

I

Miraculously wised-up
like me, but better naveled in patient
selfless humility,
I wait outside your mansion
in an ebony Dino Ferrari
while digital exclusion devices
monitor my customized hardware.

We have both of us left our arcana –
you the Stations of the Cross
and I a post-famous memorabilia.
Your white palatial on the hill
vamps a purple neon cross,
we add storylines to our lives
as a posthumous corona.

I came here on reconnaissance
knowing our much in common.
        Death
    I heard you say
        is
        the
easiest forgiven.

If I got out of the car
I'd dematerialize. Angels
are in an ordinary blood-drop,
as well as telekinetic presence.

        Jesus
    loves Elvis loves
        Jesus

is logoed on my registration plates.
Let it be accepted in heaven
where angels and lions lie down together.

II

Protector Sir of my mother,
I would ask of you the signally impossible,
her on day-leave from heaven
in a blue gown by St Laurent,
facialled and twenty years younger
than her unfacelifted state in passing

      over.
Remember her
as I do on mental television,
memory-viewing that's never fuzzy.
Even the sectioned invite weekend-leave
from remorseless institutions.
Nothing goes right without her
her black-eyed flame-orange tulips
     have failed
again, like my damage on tour,
motory dysfunctions, amnesia fogs
trip-hoppish blackout pockets.

    Special
is who we are. Your comeback tour's
still awaiting. Mine goes mega-constructed
    into passé opprobrium,

flash paste on my brocade jackets,
my funeral rites rewritten
with each burnt number each
new derision.

    Sir
    where
    Sir

do I kick the door in to revelation?
Mother's roomed up in your mansion
opportunistically in Room 425;
a hazardly apocalyptic guess
tells me she'll be cooking later
to keep her dead Elvis alive.

III

Dear Logos
word elo-
cutionist Christ
the first
lyricist, songwriter
to desert bands –
specious Charles Manson
cultically murdered
drug-screeded Gram Parsons
coopted into swastikaed
acid delusions,
it's a chiliastic
reverence has me
keep with old maudits
like Mahalia Jackson,
Bessie Smith, John Lee Hooker,
black blues on Beale Street
in a sonic coffin.
Dear Uppermost Blue
in revisionist
poppish genealogy,
there's a basement somewhere
in which music lives
like a digital river
and a blind pianist
a sunglasses-screened Ray Charles
listens and notates
smoky blue elegies.
I'll re-enter that house
it's your high-tech studio
and strip to beginnings
chthonically root
on a black slave ladder
verticalized in the stars.
Dear whatever
I need a music transfusion
I will take off my shirt
and go out to the desert
and wait in the silence
for inspiration.

IV

Dear Sir,

My mama taught me to be respectfully courteous. Someone's corrected these letters for me, but they're still sent in confidence.

As you know, Sir, I'm a compulsive collector of badges. They're like a little galaxy I spread on my counterpane. I collect police badges. I took my Memphis duty badge to a local jeweller to be embellished with rubies and diamonds. I like to be invested with the authority they provide. I court them like brooches.

I would like to tell you a story. A friend of mine, a guy from a showroom, fell in love with an angel. He met her one night when he was sitting in his car in the middle of a field. It was, he said, a night full of stars dropping out of space. He didn't know why he had felt compelled to park in the wilderness. But once he was there, he found himself liking the place and its silence.

He'd been parked there about an hour, when a girl wearing a see-through white dress floated over the field towards him. She had short black hair like a boy and walked like a model on a runway. She told my friend that she had known him for three thousand years through various reincarnational mutations. She spoke whatever the language she encountered.

She got in the passenger door and sat down beside him. She said, 'The dead provide me with lovers, but I'm alone. Mostly the right contact's impossible. Do you remember what it is like to be dead and in love with someone who's alive? Or have you forgotten? I'm here to remind you of the impossible. It's the worst sort of heartbreak. Get Elvis to sing a song about it.'

My friend thought he was dreaming. The girl had vanished, but not before she had left behind her a scintillating angel badge. The little brooch contained a name and her planetary serial code. It's too bright to be looked at, but, Sir, I long to have one of these in my possession. Send me an angel badge this side of heaven.

V

Moodily lugubrious escapee
twice post-deleted by fifties/sixties
metamorphic pop culture

it's a biographized outro
I attend to in the studio
my voice lacking the glassine shine

of a leggily seamed stocking.
From Elvis Presley Boulevard
to viewing Gladys's embalmed body

describes my circumscribed parameters.
I read my mother necrophilically,
nose, lips and little fan-shaped feet,

a seductive artefact.
Ruins – we're both premature shut-downs
are harder to silence – no one believes

in so fast an eclipsed mortality.
Youth is the one in a car crash
who returns as a legend for ever.

Over it all there's thunder
bassooned at midday for our passing
and a funeral prolonged for centuries

chaptered by websites and fanzines,
and these chisel-toed black loafers
I will wear at the silent end.

FOOD

Elvis Eyes a Jam Donut

Scurfily sugared meteorite,
a discoid jam-popper,
splitting its carbohydrate sides

like Mae West a zipper,
the thing's a sugar invert, feeds
on strawberry moisturizer

and has a trumpeter's cheeks.
Its maroony coil's
the show-stopper tease,

the compressed parachute
he anticipates opening.
His tongue patrols the surface

suctioning cubist granules
doing ghost-cunnilingus
or planetary reconnaissance

before the big burst.
Another three are back up
for repeat play taste buds.

E tickles his gustation
like a cat plays a mouse
before its fangs rip.

The donut's temptation,
almost mamillary
bopping to his palate.

Now he cantilevers
the promise in his hand
negotiates a gash

that keeps the jam intact
juicy revelation
to run red on his lips.

Junk-food Junkie

The man's a cheeseburger mausoleum,
an appetent contortionist
snake-bloated on cholesteroled junk,

intestinal-roomy as a silo
housing a grain harvest: he'll eat his way
through bear-sized stacks of burgers and French fries,

a deconstructing monument
of sinuous bacon-eddies in fat.
Heroic eating in the present tense,

no grammar to his bite, he gristles all
unpalatably hexed inedibles
into a stomach-vault for safe-keeping,

a colonic labyrinth to a tomb
of decomposing treasure. Elvis eats
proportionate to fame and limo-size

mashed potatoes, pork chops, cornbread, compact
ice creams big as Jayne Mansfield's tits,
kitchen-cut peanut butter quadrangles,

tyre-size Spanish omelettes, a butter rinse
on everything, a greasy slick.
He chews for three: dead mother and dead twin

are fibred in his chicken. He lies back:
his dead are happy and crème caramel
stays on his taste buds like the scent of fern.

Burgers

The one-hander shaped for rapacious bite,
hamburg steak wedged into a bun
as though the bread had open jaws,

salival palate like the human tongue
digging into cholesteroled fry.
Elvis at ten would walk three heat-walled miles
to Dudie's Diner, tranced there by his need
to cram and know the solid high

of something surreptitious, like store theft.
Early obsessed, he bit half-moons
from chilli glazing, upper-molared cheese

and coffined the chemical wack.
The Graceland burger was two buns deep fried,
browned in a half-stick of butter,
the burnt beef weighing a full pound

of how to stage arterial end.
Elvis became a burger mass,
an interiorized cheese continent,
a man dictated to by mayonnaise

exciting on a nether lip.
A Palm Beach Burger dollop-topped
with auroral pimento held the throne
for liquidation in three bites,

lolling against a Cadillac
or rucked in satin sheets. Teenager kicks
from fifties liberation, Elvis stayed
with junk food's oozing credibility

to be a modern fad, quick hit
into the taste buds, and the grab renewed
each time he pushed to have the meat part fit.

Fool's Gold Loafs

A house that caves in at his bite,
voluminous insides filler
pounded with toxins, gristle script

written into the gut. One pound bacon,
Smucker's grape jelly, shored peanut butter,
the whole funeralled in a Viking ship

hollowed from an Italian loaf.
Elvis orders sandwiches interjet,
the artefacts delivered from Denver

as Bible-sized catering masonry,
a barn or outhouse to the throat,
unresilient bread-shoulder.

They're his preoccupation. Scrunchy wacks.
Suburbs to sandwich culture, extensions
to how the stomach fits input

and basks in pregnant gluttony.
He digests conurbations. When he bloats
its somnolent euphoria.

It's how the butter crawls inside his mouth
entices his tongue
to tie laces. Mayonnaise

is an identifiable afterthought.
His need is proven, three as an intro
to filling the round world's imagined corners.

Elvis Picks at Turkish Delight

Baby
I'm suspicious
it's so delicious
a cubist bonbon
tastes like candy

Baby
I've a truck-
driver's need to tuck
in, it's the lemon
tincture throws me

Baby
I'm a cutie
courting a sweetie
a harem delight
voluptuous houri

Baby
I tongue it
as a plaudit
lick off the sugar
assiduously

Baby
I'm so vicious
and salacious
biting its haunches
voraciously

Baby
it's a neat pink
teaches you to think
it's the colour
of Campari

Baby
it has square toes
like a promo-
species of exotic
confectionary

Baby
I can eat
its pink suede feet
paste it to a mush
deliberately

Baby
I measure
my sweet pleasure
this little number's
rather teasy

Baby
I've a taste
for the fast and the chaste
this one undulates
cheekily

Baby
it's an art
to win a soft heart
savour the flavour
defiantly

Baby
I'm alacritous
at nibbling gelatinous
perfumed froufrous
lasciviously

Baby
I've got peepers
for more than sleepers
this courtesan's
my reality

Elvis Dopes

An Acapulco weed's acrid halo
fuzzes his stoned alumni. Nervy grass
bouffanting thought, air-
cushioning noodlish tangles
of inner discourse. Elvis drags

the coarse earth intake squintily
then comes up reaching for his space
like a scuba diver shot up
from a translucently turquoise
lagoon window

head-butted into spray.
The party orgies joints
exhaling a smoke scaffolding
a slow dispersal blue
platform of ocean fog.

A second, a third haul
of heavily furred dope
nettles in his diaphragm
tastes of rotting hemp
bangs his head out fuzzily

and dumps him on the port
carpet's sombre Octobering.
He dissociates from dope-heads
and their freaky garrulity
isolates himself with space-junk

barbiturates, stays solitary,
aerosols every Graceland room
to scrub weed traces, leaves them twine
into a free-love spaghetti
of bodies knitted on the floor.

Elvis Hikes a Raspberry Ripple

Pizzicato with a spoon
on the camel's raspberry hump
a glacial vanilla dune
syrupy with red lacquer
moon dug for taste deposits,
the new Emperor of ice cream
applies brake pads to his greed
sculpts the shock-impacted shards
to half-moons, teases two or three
into a cumulus parcel
and savours flavours as they dab
the palate like instant-hit snow
dissolving on a warm surface.
Assembling, disassembling banks
of cloud-ceilinged confection
Elvis looks philosophic
separating the raspberry
from maple and vanilla seams,
eyes closed when the solution
satisfies with a high note
prickly in its saucy tang.
He spades the camel's triple hump
to a singular hairdo,
a diminishing page cut
liquidated at a gulp
distended like a muscle.
Now he sits contemplative
picking residual granules
from recessed corners, treads his lips,
looks vulnerably unsatisfied,
waiting for someone to mother
instinctual craving for a second.

Elvis Spoons a Strawberry Jelly

The patted wobble's quakish swing,
is like a beach-thronged Rio belle's
unashamed stiletto wiggle

under wide cerulean skies.
Elvis spoonbacks gelatinous
red volume, wimpish pasty stuff,

windowed like amber, cloudy too
with a dormant opacity.
A ruby that's mouth soluble.

The jelly's buttressed from the mould,
a fortress presenting blindside,
maroonish institution.

Elvis scales a slippery crag,
the gelled mass resisting at first
like an unruly hair parting.

He solids in, persistent dig
getting a cube on leverage.
It wriggles eels inside the mouth,

no flyover to the gullet.
The thing won't stabilize, it shifts
directions like a waterbed.

He flippers in adroitly skilled
at taming perverse gradient
and stays the landslide's ripply swish.

He finds a pivotal spoonhold
and works at it like a masseur
kneading lazy curvature.

The castle's deconstructed fast,
a little flag lies in the dish
pocketed by the conquerer.

WHEN IT RAINS,
IT REALLY POURS

When It Rains, It Really Pours

Someone in black, won't turn around.
Cadential footsteps disorder
the alley's collecting silence,
bottled rainy colloquy,
blue and red neons aquariumed
in rainy shine.
                That somebody's
storyless if he stays back turned
facing the reverse of things,
a pimp, a loser, stray
loner, a Raymond Chandler theme
enigmatizing night-walking
as though he'll stop and find the key
turned tarnished in a puddle.
The man dialogues with himself,
a sleepwalker's sophistry
to object-cruise, and fixated
return to a departure point.
His blue hair's rain-gelled, backcombed strands
collapsed like tulips in a bowl
presenting downturned microphones.
He's searchily preoccupied
and could be looking for a flat
visited circa 1959,
a Moulin Rouge dancer's dope lair,
walls tessellated with pin-ups.
He stands shoulders hunched in the rain,
a nocturnal revenant
returned,
                you hear it in his tread,

exact deliberation, exact spot,
although it never enters time,

this cameo of Elvis, Elvis dead.

Just Coincidental, Baby

Freeze-framed a moment on a Harley Davidson –
Elvis in leather tracks the pool,
no variant to his clockwise thrust
around and around as though he's lost
the mouse to reprogramme a thought,

as though gravity's circular,
binding him to monotony.
Priscilla pinks a chandelier
and spectatorially observes the cat
as virtualized; a walk-in from a film,

the image buffed, her lover dead.
He's so live-wire defensive to her touch
she can't get near for resentment.
The .45 automatic tucked in his belt's
a reminder a freak brainstorm

might have him blow out on the lot.
Her vampy overkill bouffants
the leopard sofa. She's rehearsed,
refrigerated, polished like a jewel,
seething to snap back into life

like crashing in the swimming pool.
Elvis is psycho in his groove,
a blackout, hands-off, truculent rebel,
so bitter that she knows there's blood
signatured on a bitten lip.

The bike's rackety, syncopated push
chews at her nerves. He stalls it dead,
downloads his anger, and she hears the crash
of metal slapping water, and the spray
settling with wet transient feet.

Dead Elvis: Pop Song for Elvis

When I bike thru the city
free in black leather
I feel like Elvis
in the red autumn weather
dead Elvis rides by me
he's a downtown courier

When I turn on the power
baby it's freaky
he's right there behind me
he's wearing gold leather
dead Elvis zips by me
he's a downtown courier

I take third right and left
again in the rain
I'm looking for Julian's
and baby it's freaky
dead Elvis rides by me
he's like Jesus in leather

When I stop at the lights
baby it's freaky
he lifts up his visor
and looks right through me
dead Elvis sits by me
he's a downtown courier

I'm hunched in black leather
with my blonde hair tied back
I don't wanta reach Julian's
I wanna ride for ever
with dead Elvis beside me
baby it's freaky

He left me lonely
disappeared in the rain
and baby it's freaky
I want him back again
I'm searching for Elvis
goodbye Julian.

Use (Benner's *The Impersonal Life*)

Spoon-fed on spiritual sherbert
Elvis reads his tatty Benner reprint,
colours the personalized gnosis

with his E-apotheosis calling.
The book's his destiny-schema,
a blueprint in which he pulls paces

on a gold cloud dusting his road,
a heroically shooed-in destiny
like Nietzsche lifted into the mountains

by the dazzle above it all.
The chosen one's a musician
who'll die when red curtains open

in a dramatically quotidian sky.
Elvis quizzes the text like a maze
and finds himself at the centre,

funhouses meditation
and canonizes Benner
as the Patron Saint of Blue Tear-Jerkers.

Grandiosity's in order;
Elvis alerts funky coincidence
into a preconceived mosaic

contrived for a rock'n'roll Knight Templar
to be the columnar spine
pointing to a revelatory star.

Elvis feeds quote from the book
to a deadpan mafia,
lies back and savours a cheroot

on a cumulus of cushions
confesses to know the truth
like a pit understands the moistened peach.

Jealousy

Burns like a slow fuse in his veins,
an off-the-wall irrationale
feeding on misconceptions,
clouded undertow,
misassessed eye contact – the volume up

and headlighted across a room.
E is so sensitive to sleight
he mind-reads alternative talk
in her emotions, builds a storm
inside his stripped-down tolerance,

a need to clear all obstacles
to ego overkill.
He wants to wind-tunnel rivals
carpet-lift the male populace
and be again the only one

alone.
He waterfalls near ornaments
into a smashed glissando,
threatens to overdose or leave
direct for anonymity

and torch the mansion
if she gobsmacks anyone
with teasy corners of a lipsticked smile.
His temper bounces off the walls
like fizzy ball lightning

and hangs blue flame.
He'd like her radiused on a chain,
a woman on a velvet leash
admiringly obsessional
drawing Cupid's hearts on his soft-toed boot.

He slams the door and wants her out,
haystacks her clothes in the red hall,
punctures her tyres with bullet holes
and tantrum-crumples on the bed
contracted to a hedgehog's spiky ball.

Boredom as Big and Blue as the Sky

A stacked blonde sashays on heels to the pool –
the archetypal fantasy made flesh,
her black Lycra bikini's tulip-sheen
bites to be skimpier than minimal –

two isosceles triangles on string…
Her leopardspot-frame sunglasses offset
a lipstick shocked out of Matisse,
her body's second-skinned with oil.

Elvis keeps indoors shattered by the light.
Nothing will please him; each new demo tape's
vapidly cocktailed MOR
poppy ingredients spool muzzily

into a black box marked Oblivion.
The soundalike singer pitches it cool,
prospecting for the King's acclaim
and segues into parody.

The Memphis Mafia attend the blonde,
her red stilettos are like objets d'art,
wineglass-stemmed heels stood on a towel,
single-legged birds in discourse there.

She deckles lipstick on a Pepsi glass,
glosses her nails inside the time-warped zone
and feels the Boss's ennui slow
all movement to a soporific trance.

Her inner noise goes dead, then blank.
She's brought a diamond-sapphire ring,
a sparkler cushioned on a tray,
a glitzy supernumerary token

of the King's absence. E is indisposed,
black-tempered behind golden doors,
taciturn, trussed in royal state
as though he's stone-cold on a sequined bier.

Dancing On Hot Red Lips, My Love

A scorchy credo's
burning love, romance
that's pepper torrid on lips cool
as any claret rose,
incendiary skin-seal
that torches a graveyard
of oval wanting, likes it hot
as the big E on a red pout,
an orange, pink or matt scarlet
around a breath-fanned
lyric-feeling forest fire.

Hey, Big Spender

Burke's florist for a double-armed
shock of Bordeaux claret roses.
Visiting angel for a green-eyed cat.

Goldsmith's Department Store. A jackdaw fling.
A raspberry-pink jumper, a velvet chair.
His hand retrieves what the eye discovers.

Lansky Brothers for satin cowboy shirts,
boots with a teapot-pointed toe.
He marries his image inside the shop.

Lowell Hayes' jewellers. He's diamonded there.
A god who crazies light from star to star.
He thumbs a sapphire cliff-face like a mountaineer.

Popular Times for vinyl, underarm slews
of freshly minted sleeves. Old analogue
warm sound fingerprints scratched like pristine ice.

The Gridiron Restaurant for fried chicken
with grits and black-eyed peas, a double scoop
the size of a customized violin.

He window-shops Cadillac display rooms.
The upholstery smells of woody cologne.
He buys for others. It's a car habit.

Sitting in an overripe strawberry chair,
snowdrifted by carriers, he's need-fed,
his cigar writing mauve calligraphy.

Tactics

Back of the garages, an oil stain broods
a viscous fascia. Upstairs
for anonymity E flakes,

pink sleeves forced out as though positioning
for handcuffs. A vitreous slab
supported by two metal sawhorses

is the confronting desk, aqueous pane
translucent as a blue lagoon.
Outside, plump testicular tomatoes

polish red on their sunny sides.
Two fat unionized raindrops
stay flat as teardropped snails against the glass.

The guys tactic his fortissimo rage,
he'd kill all rivals, freeze the years,
be monumentally singular.

Elvis has turned wacko predictable,
his doodad and bijou counter-grab
have left him unappeased. He sprays out jewels

like accidental miracles
to traffic wardens. Now he's glucose-dead
and threatens disarrangement of the tour.

The drama's impromptu. A white heat hour's
lessened by teen-like sulks, as though his mood
stood in a basin of cool tap water.

Songwriters

A conflictual duo,
one's bleached-out sneakers
rubber the raised floor's
mahogany veneer.

The other's purple fedora
is occiput-clamped
like a mauve sorbet
true to its mould.

The upright Jack Daniel's
keeps missing a level
goes half to a quarter
colour of blond freckles.

The sheet music's shirty
scored with club-footed crotchets,
as though a Dalmatian
was ironed out flat.

The lyric's a list song
the bridge pods regret
for phrasing to coax out
the blue-hearted nut.

A chanson noire
for aural shiver,
the tempo's scare-dare poppy
as a lemony demo.

The interfaced couple
order in bagels;
the hook needs facelifting
and low-calorie consonants.

Nocturnally windowed
the city swims in
like an asteroid shower
eruptive with dazzle.

They work through the night
like cutting a suit

fitting the pieces
for interpretive voice.

It's seamless at dawn,
pins held in the teeth,
a new song tailored
for figurative breath.

Eat Your Heart Out

He'll have your taste buds thirsty
for guava or mango
or a buttocks-shaped strawberry
with a torrid summer heart,
any kind of citric tango

cocktailed with aphromania
as his pin-up does big eyes
late night in your room.
You'll dance to funky moonlight
as it windows lunar grooves,

Elvis looking rainy-hearted
on old glossy sleeves
the vinyl a mortuary
of scratches like a kitten
snagging at an arm...

He's frozen by the shutter
circa 1960
circumspectly deferential
that he's being photographed
as a cool-cat stunner

up-posing Valentino,
a blue heart in his mouth.
You'll want to lose and die
and not succeed and win
and feel the blade open

your heart like a key
Elvis at the centre
of a nocturnal ruin
framed there for ever
unattainably.

Sweet Sister Elvis

The patron saint of mothers, all sweethearts
   in shocking pink
lipstick. Sisterly solicitous
to women who feminize men,
punctilious with mealtimes, always there
   to mollify a hurt, forgive
a calculated shout-out wrong.
 He sisters their capacities
to unfailingly right an injury
   done by a lover or a friend,
and their resurrectional properties
   to rejuvenate a floored pink sweater,
a semi-ruined, button-widowed shirt.
   He celebrates the selflessness
that has them live outside themselves
   dependably attentive to each need
like analgesics for a flu, chocolate
   to sweeten medicines, white socks
produced impromptu for a sudden date.
    He authorizes praise
for their remembrance of birthdays, their eye
   for locating a lost paper
or sewing on a button with blue thread
   to match a cobalt sleeve.
He sanctifies their kitchen miracles
   their implanting geniis in cakes
whose eyes are sometimes cherries, sometimes dates.
   He's the protector of the wrong
committed on them by husbands,
    desanctifiers of female mystique,
the insensitive to a Guerlain scent,
   the inattentive to a dress,
brutal dismissers of a snakeskin shoe.
    He consolidates how they walk
and talk of little things, but remain strong
    and earthed no matter their distress
at being subjugated to male speak.
   He qualifies mothers as first,
acclaims their god-sent sacrificial love
   and appoints roses as custodians
of their benevolent, but broken hearts.

Losing Faith

Something is missing, grassroots surety,
instinctual comfort in familiar things,
the black-holed absence swallowing a past

in which he owned to an identity
private as thought, a blush-proof being there.
He monologues a chosen fan on loss,

the halls of fame are like a mortuary
in which his innocence is tagged on slab
like a trussed bundle at a poulterer's.

The blue lights snow at zero freeze.
His pre-star pristinity under wraps,
he tries repeatedly to wake the youth.

He sweats misgivings to the abashed girl.
God's moved, he says, to another address,
a mansion out of bounds to the famous.

Rhinoplasty's resolved his acne scars.
He talks of bad luck as incipient,
karmic revenge rusting his Cadillacs.

He'll catch the last train out anonymous
to find himself, he tells her, abdicate
a red silk cushion on a purple throne.

He stands back facing her, hands to the wall,
like someone frisked for weapons, then swings round,
pleadingly anguished to be left alone.

YOU'LL BE THE
DEATH OF ME

You'll Be the Death (of Me)

It's a fan's day, a parenthetical
strawberry-bite at shared glamour.
Elvis outfits Melissa's girlie probe
with insightful two-liners – stabs
at a star's eagle-summited kudos

to a blonde wannabe diva.
He autographs her teddy bear's
cinnamon-coloured jugular,
loops ostentatious flourishes
across gloss-surfaced record sleeves

and dips his straw as a second feed
into her pink milk shake.
Melissa's lactic ecstasy
has her drop a cobalt eyelash
like an offending blue bottle

in the drink's frothy polo-neck.
Elvis's laughter punches gales
through Melissa's shocked demeanour.
He cups the eyelash like an entomologist
bopping with a rare exhibit.

Elvis footsies with her high heels
parting them under the table.
Melissa blips out of orbit
feeling his foot as a wedge
act how their bodies would fit.

She goes squishily pink-hearted
at his concupiscence.
Elvis talks of his gold-maned horse,
its windy meteored arc
responsive to heroic mount.

She ends the date with his number
indigoed on her wrist.
He jets out the next day for big-time grind,
remembers her name in the show
as he croons, 'Always on My Mind'.

Always On My Mind

A black slip on the bed, her hair
an unpinned beehive's lacquered cone,
a patisserie turban swirl
is peroxided sixties-blonde.
The mirrored ceiling eyes her flash

predictable Chanel dabbings...
1059 Bellagio Road:
he's out, and so she commandeers
the bedroom's glass mausoleum,

its vacuous, museumed opulence
outerspaced in a cavernous
Hollywood-style interior, ersatz
1920s mansion. She paints her nails

rouge-noir; the colour of hot raspberries.
The King's out biking with the boys,
their convoyed Harley Davidsons
blazing a sonic tunnel through the hills,
an open-throttle thunder, sleek leather

posse of speed-age dissidents
burning a scorching trail into the sun.
She revels in luxuriating quiet,
as though the house stretched like a cat
contracting into sunny sleep.

Three shirts, a Bible, biffed script on the floor,
she retrieves items lovingly,
knowing she's here today, gone tomorrow,
another green-eyed pussycat
sashaying through his life on red spike heels.

She curls unto the mould his body left
in satin sheets, strums a guitar,
and sits there saucered by a rakish hat.

Funky Exotica

There's a funky piranha
eats ginseng and guarana
    in Elvis's tank.

There's an ape in a fun-wig
purple as a split fig
    in Elvis's zoo.

There's a brain-fazed astronaut
savouring sauerkraut
    on Elvis's tomb.

There's a mouse with maracas
nibbling crisp crackers
    in Elvis's lap.

There's a cat who's a diva
eyes made up like Shiva
    on Elvis's bed.

There's a violet-eyed beautician
who's a high-tech mortician
    in Elvis's bath.

There's a sunset-plumaged parrot
the colour of a carrot
    on Elvis's perch.

There's a colon-irrigator
who's wearing alligator
    in Elvis's chair.

There's a dyed pink Chihuahua
sipping chilled tequila
    from Elvis's glass.

There's a time-fazed pilot
eating a black violet
    with Elvis's spoon.

There's a loony with a gun
shooting holes through the sun
    with Elvis's aim.

Pink Sapphire

A matcher to a soap-pink Cadillac,
a bijou reward to his anima,

self-excess apotheosis
feminized by his difference,

it's a coveted hybrid
a transgender stone in his jewellery stash

worn as a shyly blushing light
the colour of cheekish rosé.

Black Sapphire

A broody thunderstorm, a mutant jewel
glowers depression on his finger,

lapidary melancholia,
colour of the death-god's cobalt feet.

Imploding blackener in a Howes claw
he orchestrates its depth-notes like a child

blood-warms an abyssal marble
then crashes it at collisional worlds.

Picture This

Dismounted in the choking harvest heat –
the wheat prairie's a frisky sea,
he waits as leader of the pack's
Harley camaraderie
to be united with his speedy gang.
He's denarrated in this frame,
roadsided, impatient to reconnect
with how the story goes, two minutes out of time
unspliceably threatening, banged alert
into isolated reality –
the shut-up human in him running scared.

Picture That

He's miles from anywhere. A Kamikaze
Jim Morrison vocal attack
glasses the airwaves, druggy contestant
to sixties eschatology.
Elvis picnics with a jean-torn gamine
and studies himself as the wounded god,
a red guitar stood at his feet
as a memorial, the raffish site
searched by a shadow dropped out of the sun
to beat around him, as he sits up-branch,
hearing his rivals riff on overkill.

Elvis Chooses Shalimar

Her name's water-soluble on his tongue,
a nineteenth-century flower, a dash
of rum quixoticizing cream,

a beauty spot pixelating a cheek.
He does telepresence all day,
aura-invader in her room,

infrared bug seeing through clothes.
It's the Baccarat bottle grabs his eye
at Goldsmith's smellies department

his chord-sampling meeting a saraband
of vanillin and opoponax,
sandalwood locution and incensesy

intimations of Scheherazade,
the belly-dancing genie in the scent
discarding chiffon veils,

arching a back in languorous citrus,
insisting with lavender notes.
Elvis goes max size with a purple bow,

a store-wrapped satin glossy on the box.
His mystery woman's at the hairdresser's,
and tented in pink towels small-talks

about a dark-haired stranger – could it be
the unpronounceable – or just a man
romancing words on a tonic spring day?

Diamonds

A jeweller's archipelago
blue-stoned at the throat
for Linda and Ginger
a necklaced galaxy,
carboniferous light
which will outlive the planet,
meaningless to Elvis
after the purchase.

Mystique

It's like a vodka shot, invisibly
translucent spirit windowed in a glass,
the perfect disappearing act.

Elvis made absence presence on the screen,
was everywhere that way ubiquitous,
and free to inhabit real time.

Garbo rinsed her blonde hair in camomile,
a sheenish trick, no bright highlights,
and made herself her only company

beneath raindropping chandeliers.
The world was like a liner lost in fog.
The crystal forest claimed her for its own.

Presley wave-functioned parallel
to placing building blocks of fame
so high around himself he couldn't see

the moment for its slight delay.
He wore a pink frilly shirt. Christ appeared
and handed him a red guitar.

Mostly he deepened into missing time,
and grew to be eponymous.
He staged elaborate funerals for himself

and poured red roses on the bed,
and stood back amazed, as the mirror framed
someone he knew accounting for the dead.

Star

Solitude's like the light trapped in a star,
matter turned in upon itself
as an event horizon. No one there.

It's like a cryogenic freeze,
off-limits seal in liquid nitrogen,
posthumous life awaiting the big thaw

back to reality; diamonds and all.
Elvis is cornered like a rhinestoned fish
lip-syncing at aquarium walls.

The windows painted black, and sealed by foil,
he lies in state on a round bed.
The TV is his sanctioned multiverse;

a cowboy rides direct into the room.
He thinks of relocating to the sun,
his image shining on the earth

as constantly transmitted brilliance.
He dyes an eyelash. Nothing's real.
A purple toy sits on a fake-fur throne,

a purple leopard with knuckle-sized spots.
It's autumn outside. Tepid fuzz.
He spoons an ice cream shaped like a pink urn.

His Las Vegas cape twinkles on the bed.
The world is very far. His feet are blue.
He'll stage a comeback, descending from clouds.

Prescription Drugs

Unquantifiably
metabolized. Dexies,
Dilaudid, codeine-
laced Hycodan syrup,
the dead King stands up.

Liquid cocaine
wads in the nostrils
Amytal, Carbrital,
Nembutal, Seconal,
the dead King stands up.

Demerol shots,
Placidyl, Quaalude,
Valmid, Valium –
hypnotics, sedatives,
the dead King stands up.

Polypharmaceutical
narcotic protocol
recreationally cocktailed
liver intolerable
the dead King stands up.

Toxic alchemical
Elavil, Aventyl,
Amytal, Sinutab
constellating metabolites
the dead King stands up.

Authorized toxicity
fists full of Tylenol
morphine predominant
degenerating fatty heart
the dead King stands up.

Uppers, downers, multiversed
pharmacists, medicos
paid for illicit scrips
with cars and dollars so
the dead King stands up.

Oh Help Me, Please, Doctor

My polypharmacy turns night to day,
the uppers, downers, hits my cells sustain,
are quanta burning in a neutron star,

the quarks and leptons of neurology.
Placidyls, Quaaludes, Nembutal and speed,
they supernova in my chemistry

and cushion me against reality.
At twelve, experience bit me like a snake,
the clean incision smelled of dead apples,

and something broody like catastrophe
waiting to show up in disordered genes.
I learnt that both sides of a fruit decay,

and death means seeing people on wavelengths
spookily parallel. When Gladys died
I bit a white moon-sized barbiturate

and never stopped swallowing on that pill.
It was my mother I metabolized
in starburst granules as a death ritual,

a chemical reunion in my blood.
I cocktail drugs, and brood inside the space
they open up, like colouring a word

with emphasis, then repeating the phrase.
I swim inside a soporific soup,
lowdown, downtown, lowlight, and sunk for good.

Elvis's Pin-ups

Brigitte Bardot's
a fantasized paramour
a bee-stung pouty ocelot
all bottom choreography
insolently sultry

Lolita-ish gamine
animalized, sulky
unlibidoed stripteaser
the opposite to Elvis's
maternal Southern belles.

Gina Lollobrigida's
S-shaped Latin figure
invites sustenuto
to his rumba fantasies,
Gina's seamed silk stockings

dusted with Arpège
are translucent as his thoughts
imaging her peppery
uptake of his charm
cushioning like moleskin.

Raquel Welch's uplift
areolas for Elvis's
left supporting hand.
Nancy Sinatra's
showbizzy tiara

or Diana Dors's
archetypal smooch
are nothing to Sophia
Loren's smoky mystique,
blood chilli-hot.

Elvis opposites
in fantasy orientation
gravitates to tempered
lugubrious Latins
with their cat-rippled charms.

Elvis Dyes His Eyelashes

The risk's potential shut-down of his sight,
the dye infiltrating the retina,

the man and image wanting harmony,
inkily dyed hair, inky eyelashes,

a bottle-black rival to bottle blondes.
He detail-frisks a solitude

deepwater as a sullen lake. The gods
wear bloody blindfolds in his dream

and hold glass buttons for eye-substitutes,
a green, a blue, a cloudy grey, a brown.

His doctor brings a scarlet rose.
They talk flashy cars, not retinitis.

The barbed-wire word's glaucoma; the big G
as diagnostic metaphor

for ivied ruins shuttered to the world
companioned by inhospitable ghosts.

Elvis grows lachrymose, thinks terminal,
increases his get-dead-quick armoury

and fads on deep-fried chocolate slabs.
His sight's 50:50 lesioned, the quirks

and frogspawn in his visual field.
He wants to stay on-line with what he sees,

resist the tunnel where the lights blow out
and darkness swallows the oncoming train.

Elvis's Anti-ageing Policies

He's liposuction flab-firmed
reconstructed. He retrieves
a year not twenty in a day
thinking Giacometti lines
as though he's just neurology
pared to a new species geek
a retro purchase on revamped
habilitation to sleek youth
testosteronal cubbish rolls
with pouty jean-torn gamines
toes making circles in the air.
Excoriated, liver-roughed
houser of toxins he's detoxed
and tucked to hide facial excess,
relaunched as a de-laurelled King,
the youthful myth
middling resentfully, half-turned
to a blueing oblivion
as exit from falling apart.
E loses to popstar
anorexics, roots solid
as any oak, defies the rules
by illicit burgering,
dreams he'll be transmogrified
to Audrey Hepburn, Sophia Loren,
or walk out of the rehab room
a sharp-featured 180lb
and stabilize as that.
A pouring laburnum's yellow
tasselled braids show in the window
before he blocks the view.
Spring's like a floral chocolate box
of blossom-heady surprises.
E looses a chin, gains a tusk
for carbohydrates, emerges
ravenous to clear a fridge,
forage for mercy foods, avoid
the mirror, imagine himself
twenty years younger, frontal flat
as a smooth-planed coffin board.

Elvis Thinks Gay

It's like a reversible car
same thing but a different fit
O Lawdy mother in a man

incest with my wounded own.
I paint my eyes better than hers
O Lawdy do mascara too

springtime myself with Paris scent
bottle unstoppered gold on black
O Lawdy sister's feeling blue

It's not opposite so it's true
loving my own as me in you
O Lawdy you in me's as good

My pink jacket outrivals hers
better on his, my ruffled shirt
O Lawdy drag's a comfort fit

I outmodel Brigitte Bardot
the woman in me's man for man
O Lawdy sequins raining down

My mother lives in a man's smile
I'll claim her by breaking back in
O Lawdy the tunnel's so dark

My looks have women jealous, men
appreciate what rivals don't
O Lawdy and I'm crying in the rain

Elvis Thinks Lesbian

Hamming it with woody cologne
Elvis thinks Mary for a day
O sisters love yourselves and not my own

Leaving men out it's right that way
excluded once, excluded twice
O sisters true love's being gay

Death on the bed is really life
two lipstick ovals meshing red
O sisters take the other for a wife

Heteros are the commonplace
they're 1 + 1, no unity
O sisters share a made-up face

True love's the right catch as same kiss
the sameness meets seamlessly
O sisters Mary is your Miss

Life's too repeat to occupy
decades of being programmed straight
O sisters teach pink wings to fly

Love between man and woman's man's
go it along a diky road
O sisters catch it as catch can

Take two silk stockings, share one seam
the leg will always fit
O sisters let me live my dream

2 Die 4

His prophylactic peaks as molten pearl.
Mutual orgasmic deaths mean 2 die 4.
The androgynous King is boy and girl.

His gross-out lubricity tries again.
The androgynous King is boy and girl.
The boulevard records limos in rain.

Mutual orgasmic deaths mean 2 die 4.
Prosthetics enhance possibilities.
An angel in suede thighboots tries the door.

The boulevard records limos in rain.
His infrared footage freeze-frames her scream.
A metal channel-zap fires through his brain.

An angel in suede thighboots tries the door.
A mink coat tents the bed. A split necklace
has raindropped emeralds across the floor.

His infrared footage freeze-frames her scream.
Prosthetics enhance possibilities.
He fighter-pilots his way through a dream.

The androgynous King is boy and girl.
He's the approved supreme riding high.
His prophylactic peaks as molten pearl.

His videotheque holds others in store.
A metal channel-zap fires through his brain.
Mutual orgasmic deaths mean 2 die 4.

Silver-barrelled Therapy

The mirror's cracked. A splinter-
chip from the mandala sticks
as verbal. Taciturnly fazed
he swallows it like stringy worm

doused in tequila.
His analyst's eyes are blue fish
swimming behind smoked glasses
in undetected flurries.

Elvis presents stacked heels
blocked on the pink chaise longue,
one-half-inch lifts in his boots
polished obsidian,

throned on the dusky corduroy.
He won't let Jesse escape
deepwater in his soul,
a drowned twin finned with grief

reproachfully hard-scaled.
Elvis won't live it all,
the integrated split.
The guilt he feels stains everything

like bruising on a strawberry.
Therapy doesn't take him where
he's windowed in the clear
like gin.

He wants to remain storyless,
no involvement
in narrative, no going back
to clear a space between the trees…

He's uncooperatively angular
to search that takes depth in.
His analyst looks up to find
the broody pointing with a gun.

The Wild Within the Tame

His roomy drawl ponders over St John;
a Bible convocation at Graceland,
Elvis repurposing Apocalypse
to fit with revelation on the stage,

professes vision as a fire-walker,
a traveller from star to star
returning as the deathless one
in a bruised mauve George Barris Cadillac,

an interspecies visitor
redeeming cities through a voice
grown indigo roots in gospel.
Elvis refers to sightings, look-in lights

skylighted over Memphis, abductees…
He's Jesus in gold pyjamas,
dispensing miracles with a chequebook,
disconsolately car-whisked out at night

to play chess on his mother's grave.
He sits there, tented in a velvet coat,
obsessed with winning Gladys back,
the night chill filigreed with rain,

his limo parked up under trees.
Fame, he will say, is like a snail's glitter,
a dazzle rubbed out underfoot.
His mother's website opens in his mind,

psychic dictation, and he's blown away
into a trance state, words coming
as though sourced on the other side.
He tunes into his fingers: he can heal.

They lead him to the gold-trimmed Stutz,
a minder on each arm. He brims with tears.
Mother is deep inside him now,
blue as the morning glory's bluest flower.

ELVIS: THE
MISSING DIARY

Messianic Confirmation (1975)

His brain hoovers at pharmaceuticals,
sea-sponges micrograms.
Lucidly intervalled
he close-encounters Jesus Christ
frying up in the kitchen –

fish, of course, popping in batter.
The bread slices are cut into crosses.
Jesus's hair is ponytailed
like a hippie's.
His ring's netlinked to posthuman helpers.

Elvis sashes his kimono –
gold dragons meteored on black.
He teleports to a chair,
the tabletop's an open rose,
immaculately claret.

Jesus closes an eye
approving of flesh texture,
the grainy fillets spit
and camber in the fat –
miracle fish from the Red Sea.

Elvis butters Jesus's bread
in gold cobbled nuggets.
He feels twenty years lighter
a surrogate messiah
the drugs cleaned from his head.

Jesus answers his netlink,
wine appears on the table
a broody Nuits-Saint-Georges
warm from an angel's hand
vintagely sacramental.

Jesus rakes the fillets over
in a flurried live crackle.
Elvis sings a cappella
a bluesy gospel number
aureoled by grace.

Crawling Leopardskin (1976)

Dysfunctional seasick balance,
he's RCA-mobiled at home,
propped up for heroic pitch
in a Gestapo-style leopard coat,
his diction furry and slurred,

his photophobia acute.
Elvis believes the coat
will come alive on padded feet
a rippling bacchante cat
fit ruby claws to his throat.

Heroically wounded on 'Hurt',
he real-things the take.
He speaks to someone not there,
an alias called Jack
about never coming back...

His temper's up for grabs
and blown out like a gun.
He's sweating in dead skin
to metaphor his state
like a big cat lies down

in the grass and is done.
He dialogues with Jack
about singing in a bar
hypeless, anonymous,
a low-profile star...

He wears the collar turned up
and his sneer turned down,
fake fur given attitude,
promenaded, royalled,
tented like a diva's gown.

He sweats through 'Moody Blue',
but won't let go the metamorphic wrap.
He's overblown his boundaries,
burst like the god's purple grape
along a ripe autumnal seam.

Love to Love You Baby

Mitsoukou lingers as a scent-striptease,
vetiver unzipping to bergamot
        cool at first
then hot,
and later on forgot.

Testosterone spiked in a booster vein
reactivates his desensitized sex
        up at first
too hot,
and later on forgot.

Loneliness eats up possibilities
of being someone other than himself
        weird at first
then hot,
and better off forgot.

Letters rain across his mauve counterpane,
the image-sippers feed like hummingbirds
        sure at first
and hot
and later on forgot.

Waiting implies a coming and an end
to waiting, nobody as somebody
        there at first
and hot
and later on forgot.

Lying down every day means standing up
in memories that activate a song
        cool at first
then hot
and later on forgot.

Suck on This (1977)

June Jaunico, Dixie
Locke, back-seated
innocence – hemlines courted by
a sippish summer breeze
coded in memory,
databased and lost.
Wilson Regis Vaughan,
Linda once compatible
Thompson, Ginger
inflammatory Alden,
Priscilla Beaulieu most
ballroomed in the heart,
Barbara Leigh, Sheila Ryan,
all superluminaries,
Anita Wood, Natalie
the same surname,
mink-coated, Jaguared,
beneficiaries of excess,
reduced to plaintive syllables
approved of by pain.
They're infrared images
recorded on time-film
inerasible contacts
intersecting with Elvis
telephone numbers
stored in the unconscious
the old and the new
pincoded there for ever,
updates typed in.
Priscilla's reproachfully
solicitous, face turned away
accusing, valedictory,
face turned around
importuning innocence.
Ends aren't reversals
they're agendaed reminders
of incompletions,
nothing put down, nothing picked up,
like the blue sea's rhythm
the wave tumbling forward broken
by the backwashed wave's opposition.

An Open Letter to the Universe (1977)

Aleph – Christ –
Omega King of rock
'n'roll, this predated obituary's
a resignation, curtain call
for red drapes, opulent vermilion,
the BIG BLACK final credits
as they showed prematurely for Gladys,
receding to vanishing point,
derealized, a sassier obit.
What we do individually's devalued,
the future's only concerned with the new
and its upcoming chartables.
Graceland's a departure lounge
for a night flight with the cabin on dimmers
unanswerable to air-traffic control,
a crewless flight through the dark
with no supportive luggage.
In Larry Geller's prompting –
the Aitareya-Upanishad
speaks of a hundred and one arteries
highwayed to the heart,
a vertical point going through the head
by way of terminal exit:
it's the final ladder to the stars.
Four electrifying years
burning the establishment down,
the rest sanctuaried in unreality,
parasitical on the past.
Posthumous hits will cruise on the airwaves
and voice-surf through beachy summers,
the tearjerker icon sustain
a heart-throb hold over women
fixing their hair in car mirrors.
The way out's through the stage door,
with no fans beehived by the car,
just a clean break,
                              a barefoot dash
without security,
running to heaven on a mirror floor.

Later Than Late (1977)

Take a piece of string
let the thing unroll
across a continent
he sings,
            coz I'm through,
freaking to his driver
as rain steps on the road.
Or take fibreoptic
filaments, start out
transmitting how a person
is the chosen one
one amongst a million
a standout in the crowd
better than Sinatra
in a black fedora
he sings,
            coz it's hard
ending alone
as rain steps on the road.
Watch a bloodline hum
like a digital river
haemoglobins and white cells
mismultiplying,
the genome breaking down –
words from a doctor
he sings,
            like an end,
personal dissolution
as rain steps on the road,
winter and summer
the same sad crooners
sit on red bar stools
singing of losers
like they've never won,
he sings,
            coz it's over,
bury us all together,
Sinatra, Bennett, Presley
the two of them in suits
and me in gold leather.

Psalm

By the waters a junk-chest
of smashed vinyl records,
black dinner plates cracked like defunctive suns.

A spill of obsolete memorabilia,
photographs signed in garnet lipstick,
mosquitoes collectivizing a double-bass

fan-blower over a sage-green puddle.
Centuries walk out on each other
in high-heel red shoes,

disconsolate as miffed autograph-hunters.
Time is wiped clean in the stars:
angels are remixed information.

A coffin's a hardware drawer
lined in pink satin,
a disposable tool rotted by rain.

If a man stands in a garden
his grief given exclamation,
his need will track upwards to the stars.

In the aspiration hope
like being plugged into the cosmic mains
a visionary neuronal aurora.

Re-sightings by still black waters,
an Elvis Presley EP flaked soggy
rippling there like a footnote to history.

FREAKY
OBSESSIONS

Freaky Obsessions

Bullet holing a scarlet Pantera
for faultily wired ignition
he gun-butts a metal ritual, barrel

haemorrhagic from misfiring:
another notch in his munitions legend,
the bodyguarded one who defuses

his minders' killing potential.
He's the do-righter absolving his guilt
for recurrently fantasized murder;

he's a catsuited karate chopper
projecting himself from a bump-surfed train roof
clean through a car's open window –

one hand on the leopardskin wheel
arresting a crash course, the other
impacting the cartel's neck vertebrae

with a clean snap register.
He lolls back on his boot heels, moulds
himself to repeat hit bravado –

the narrative splashy as blood
in the reality of telling.
Elvis's instincts are movie-framed

as he turns away from the car
writes out a cheque for the damage
and bangs his fist on the hood.

Home on the Farm (1970)

He's twitchy in the copperish-red haze,
days out of tour, Octoberish
designs to un-Elvis himself

in rootlessness, kick free a name
and biff chestnuts radiused around a tree,
each dumped arrival polished like a cricket ball.

Elvis speaks Miracle Network with Jim.
He plans to underground identity,
embrace the Church of Angels Born on Earth

and learn to sit with meditation space
inside his feeling precinct. A year out
will magic-carpet hop the andropausal

dumps, the heavy-duty blues.
He'll be a nimbused pixelgraph
to fan-based fantasy,

an absence fed by sky-highed record sales.
They talk looking into the mist's
translucency of tulle shawls;

leaves look like they've been soaked in wine,
blackcurrant-coloured claret.
Jim's Archangel to the cult's neophytes

and first disbanding of identity.
His spirit-morphing helps reshape
luminous mind-designs.

Jim catches a parachuting black leaf
and points to tendril, petiole,
the infrastructural skeleton,

and metaphors comparison
to psychic highways – Elvis's are clear,
the small roads travelled leading to the whole.

Divorce

Contracted blood money. He'd kill Mike Stone,
the wounded King's decree is spit and shoot
as volatile appeasement of his pain.
The telephone's a ripped-out liana.
He spraycans Day-Glo threats across the wall

and rages at her infidelity,
the girl he's cheated on from a perverse
miscalculated sense of loyalty –
he keeps her as the inviolable one,
and feeds his kicks on coming back to her

in brutally duplicitous penance.
She's gone, and freedom hurts without restraint.
His threats obscenely free associate,
Priscilla's shacked in Pacific Palisades
duetting with her karate icon,

while Elvis snake-bloats on triple French fries
and mind-schemes homicidal bloodlettings.
At night, he shifts from floodlit room to room
obsessed she's there in hiding, white on white,
contritely naked in a tiara…

His wounded machismo finds no respite
in vindicatory back-up from the boys.
A sapphire earring's underlit night sky,
a rack of frosty silks, marabou pumps,
are a reminder trail like face powder

still granulated on a red cushion
of her inflammable need to want out.
He bumps into his guilt and runs away
as though a forest fire made savage tracks
and singed his hammered break towards the road…

His past is torn along a jagged seam.
He'll substitute dumb bimbos for his doll,
grow bitter from betrayal, recluse himself
inside a Bible, looking for a love
that burns so bright it's unconditional.

White House Visit

December's mineral sparkle dusts with frost.
A random ice hexagonal
parachutes as beginning snow

before the air turns fizzy diamond.
E flight-hops to the White House unannounced,
his imperial purple crushed-velvet suit

offensive to Nixon's sobriety.
The chintzy Oval Office smells of cigars,
the desk draped by a tulip field of flags,

a clashy panoply.
Nixon chews on E's gunning objective
to chase a drug youth to the lion's jaws…

E's confirmed undercover. Both men freeze.
A glowering fire's orange vitality
goes sparky in the grate. Elvis's badge,

a BNDD, brooches in his hand.
His gift to Nixon's cool metal,
a veteran war killer Colt .45

circa 1918. No gelling space,
the two men separate. Elvis cocktails
a secret deposition in his mind,

a White House coup, a string stacked slow-burner
by way of an acceptance cadenza.
He goes out to a polka-dotted sky,

a compact cushioning of snow.
He's face down-turned dejected, badge and all,
limoed away into a chocolate dusk.

It Could Be Him (1972)

Detained for questioning,
a blood-mosquito sipping at a vein
for investigative read-out
displayed on micro-screen,
the indexed drugs identified
in quantitative micrograms,
a teenie's autumn-coloured hair
draped on a leopard-print collar,
roomed there beside him –
out of it –

the nightmare colouring
to three shades grey
all over shampooed
consistency, and snapping out of it –
reality, the metal bite
of being led away
into a 6 x 8

conclusively asphyxiating cell.

Guns

Obsessive weaponry. His hand takes note
of weight needed to murder. Wrist-
bone flex. A counterphobic thrust ·
to suicide, mock OTT
pretensions to the red-mouthed myth

of dying younger than one's death,
auto-blasted out on black silk pillows
in a star-pampered scarlet suite.

His yellow Didamasa Pantera
lemons outside Kerr's Sporting Goods.
E's gun fetish itches mid-brain,
he magnetizes peculiar metal,

body-holds it as killer prosthetics.
Black caped, ebony walking cane
dandifying his kitsch, he reads the stock
as blue snub-nosed familiars,
lethal mouthpieces for a psychopath...

His autocratic mania thrills
at gun-handle contact.
A James Bond Biretta automatic,
a Mauser Luger glow machine-pistol

are leather-cased into his 265.
He Nazifies his fantasies,
abrupt kill at the speed of thought,
heroics acclaimed by a dumbstruck blonde.

He's the King of the castled armoury,
the badge-appointed undercover shot,
polishing a Sten gun with silk panties,

playing it cool, and playing it hot.

Elvis Does some Coffin-testing

He's like a sandwich-filler, laid back flat
on cherry satin boards.
It's meditational initiation,

a yogic posture for last rites
when roses splash red autumn on a grave
as though they're lipsticked to the spot.

His prediction's an early death,
youth as a glass rained into from a height
as soon evaporated.

The fit's tailored like breath to the nostrils,
exact aplomb and countenance,
his head still chemistried with noise.

Elvis primes up at the undertaker's
in shrink-wrap privacy. The sprayed gold lid
twinkles with shimmied fairy lights.

His strongbox size is overlarge.
He backfloats in a sack-black room,
the dark creating luminosity.

It's like the shut-tight snailshell feel
of surfing a flotation tank,
a mind-bending virtuality.

He sweats it out, a gamy thing
before switches are thrown. Revitalized,
he sees the light inside like a lemon

shine livid as flat Warhol paint.
He's driven back to Graceland like someone
emitting sparks each time he dusts his coat.

Purple Haze

Where his aunt should be, a purple shadow
roomy as a refrigerator pools
a weight-specific density,
a voluminously floored block
which lifts a right hand with his own
in synchronistic fluency,
bruised, projectile diagonal
flopping back from the vertical
in search of full-fat building blocks
of butter, ham and wedgy cheese.
The ripply shadow does wobblies
according to his stand or sit
endeavours. Now it's like a boat
staining its berth indigo-black
and deepening like a jelly in its mould.
He'd like to split from the binary bulk,
and can't be sure if it's his aunt
or a new carpet square, or him
pretending he's a polar bear
walked flat, or a newfangled safe
hauled in and left for fixturing.
He's confused about being there
unaided, drug-cloudy, shooed-in
by compulsion. He stamps the mass,
but can't erase its persistent purple
flotation. It's cheese-nuggety
as though tailored to accumulate grit.
He keeps on dropping stuffy things,
a food-cram jigsawed on the floor.
He stands up and the thing's square on.
He's certain it's his aunt gone dumb,
and leaves the room thinking purple, purple,
a purple shaving spot, a purple thumb.

Elvis Counsels David and Angela Bowie

They're homaged, legs crossed in the Trophy Room.
He's an emaciated drag-Dietrich
camped into scarlet high-heel boots,

coke-paranoid, occulted, fidgety,
his geisha's make-up moonscaped as blue dust.
She's morphed herself into his counterpart,

a microed leggy androgyne,
the patron saint of gender crossovers.
Elvis is age-shy, shrinkingly obese,

his Southern patriarch's diplomacy
cooling their octane disputes. She's afraid
he's vampirized the image metamorphoses

she protoed for his bi/gay repertoire.
She'd like to copyright the her in him,
barcode her influence. They're twin messiahs

contending for a freakish red-haired cult.
They're both availably promiscuous
and jealous of the other's liberty.

Elvis seems grandiosely sagacious.
He pours the Scotch whisky like tea
into their endlessly depleted tumblers.

Nothing's resolved. She claims he's the black fruit
corrupting her. She spits him out,
but likes the tinctured poison on her tongue.

She storms outside. He follows drunk.
His black fedora's like an undertaker's hat.
Their stretch limo limps off down Heartbreak Road.

Detox: Baptist Hospital

He's hepatitis bloated, liver ruined,
corticosteroids excessed in his cells.
He's like a beached, chemically crippled fish,

a junkified boy mitting pills
instead of poison-coated sweets;
the lie digesting in himself
as underworlded habit. Hit. Forget.

All of those private jettings to LA
Demerol got on Wilshire Boulevard
pharmacist-sized jars stashed away,
capsuled confection of downers

enough to blanket a pink elephant.
They lift them out like funeral urns
stored in a sacerdotal vault
download his Graceland pharmacy,
his pact with cocktailed altered states,

this man whose death wish cooks in a gene soup.
He's internally stripped of chemicals,
as though someone looted a jeweller's tray

and prized out emeralds, sapphires,
lifted them from a velvet bed.
He struggles with the shrinks. They'd methadone
his system into come-down cure,

a street user's rehab. He scores inside,
but turns the spiral round, retrieves
a patchily depressed equilibrium,
gets out, continues with the lie,

believing in his luck, hide like an elephant
no bullet kills stampeding through the rain.

Boulevard of Broken Dreams

Elvis in leopardskin frogs through the rain.
A naked cutie shoulder-trails her coat

and ball-bearing walks on mauve stilettos.
Her buttocks tattoo reads Phobos/Deimos –

the filling station Martian moons.
She's called Elvissa in his trance-fielding,

her jet-black hairdo set in double quotes.
Her VR Chihuahuas mouse in and out.

His dream's like zero gravity.
A hearse sleeks by as disinformation.

The distance never narrows. Underfoot,
glass crackles like he walked on red Mars rocks.

Ruby as Big as Dracula's Heart

Elvis's use-up power's vampirical.
His family's psyched like Manson's, spirit-drained

to feed consumptive ego. Faxy lives
telepresent to serve the King.

His frying pan's the size of God.
Omelettes blotch there like suns, and Dracula

rises in red conical flames,
Elvis learns from the maestro's blood-sampling

a road to acquisitive power.
Graceland's his own gothic laboratory,

his identityless devotees
are transfusable to his rebus gain.

Women are shimmy-imageries,
jewellery to decorate his feminine.

His heart's a craggy gothic stack
a chateau lit for devilry.

His omelette's full of gobbled souls.
Elvis gains pounds from expendable lives.

His sycophants are psi-hexed refugees
assembled round the bed to stake his heart.

Ouch My Heart is Breaking

Howz it I tie up and shoot
or have shot in a recessed vein
trade-name pharmacy morphine
like a bruised Billie Holiday
and habity *poètes maudit*
Sassy and Dinah Washington
whitening into a slow freeze
and in denial of my need?
Ouch the needle registers
rushes my brain chemistry
and I'm deep-sea in the space
occupied as aftermath,
hit high on an August day,
dressed in a black satin shirt,
ready to OD or wake
to the funeral of my youth.

Last Star Out

An instant of pure being –
psycho-glitter psychicized
like a thistle's blowball halo
filigreed, the luminous
coming on in him direct,
spontaneous, instantaneous,
bottoming out from household blues
roomed up oppressively all day,
his picking up acoustically
with a living room 'Blue Suede Shoes',
a pre-punk impromptu 'Hound Dog',
the boys gustoed in hot pursuit
Sinatra on the stereo
with his Big Apple barroom talk
and overhead an orange moon
propositioning love the way
it always seems an up there star.

BLACK LIMO BLUES

Elvis Presley at Forty

The walls are black fake suede in buttoned strips,
a bedroom like a car's interior
sealed off as though the King's already dead,
his body grown to be an elephant's,
a creature out of climate in the South.
He sits in state on a red coverlet,
nursing an automatic, levels it,
and blasts a wall-pinned photograph
between the eyes. He'd reinvent himself,
retrieve the snake-hipped Lizard King
if he could find a way to kick
the drugs that snow into his brain.
He's draped the mirrors so his eyes won't meet
the facially rotund, 20-stone hulk
inhabiting his room. Gold pyjamas,
hair blacker than a funeral car.
A rhinestoned, Las Vegas gladiator,
he lives inside that time warp, clings to fame
like someone holding with both hands
to the roof of a speeding train.
He's lonely in decline. Each new decade
invalidates his image. When he eats,
he puts a coating on despair,
a cheeseburger cushion over the drop.
He spades into his sixth banana split,
then fires a second shot to have an aide
come running to his room. It's always night
inside and out for him, a night
that leads to his dead mother, and she waits
to guide him through a long tunnel
into the greater light. He waves to her,
and she salutes him with a torch.
He's happy now. The gold discs on his wall
are blazing planets, and his forty years
slow for a moment like an animal
dropped to the dust to lick its hurt,
or Gladys all those years ago
holding back tears, sending him off on tour,
crying through laughter on the Graceland porch.

Christmas at Graceland

Elvis golf-carts from room to room,
his skid-marks cleating a black marble floor
so licked a chandelier drips

reflections in jet like a tree a lake.
The tree's a tinselled drag-queen's crown
a bushy Alp with frosted arms

dazzled against red velvet drapes.
The three magi have touched in from the stars,
a pause in interplanetary travel,

helmets and systems left out in the hall.
A glitter-spectacular foil affair,
a card-fan pleated on a baize table

reads out a quint flush of five hearts.
The new day's like molecular building blocks
arranged into a synthy hologram.

Presents arrive in humpbacked sacks,
silver and red and gold wrappings
too many to be sorted by his hand.

Outside, the snow's backdropped scenario
lends high ethereality
to blue abstracted air.

Elvis is reverentially festive
the brightness in his mood trapped from a star
and numinous inside his heart.

A messenger comes to the gates,
requesting her child's taken in,
then walks coatless into the gelid town.

The First Time Ever (I Saw Your Face)

Eventful freeze along the spine.
Roberta Flack's big spaces round her words
are meditations in a song
opening and closing doors on mystery;

the once known unrepeatable
entry-point to another's life,
exchange of everything, a mutually
experienced identity – the eyes
brimming with neural galaxies;

the separation loud with energies.
Elvis makes a visceral grab
at revisioning love, opening his arms
to somebody who knows his all

pre-verbally, who lives like rain
falling into his thoughts, and leaves
an auric perfume on the air,
a rumba twist of Shalimar...

He wants to signature the hit,
invest it with his colouring,
and through the song claim love for real,
as though he sang into her eyes
and watched them brim with blue diamonds.

He afterglows the record's end,
and stores each phrase in memory,
protects it like a secret found
and fed by hand, kept in the heart,
and later lifted into sound.

Backstage Fights

Elvis lacks veins for a punched booster shot.
His body's a disaster site,
its neural highways misinformed by drugs.
He's show-maintained; golf-carted to the stage

and framed there like a building block
huge volume dinosauring on the boards.
He's tubed off by a corporate vampire,
singing to lose his money like loose rain…

A parasitical assemblage feeds
on every concert's twice-disputed cheque,
the singer's unsurefooted looty haul
burnt in illicit stashings, hotels, jewels…

His live-in puts him up against the wall:
she's packed, and smouldering gorgeous
and threatens him with a clean-up or out
impassioned directive, a do-or-die

invective, pitched hysterical
against his shifty flat-refusal means
to ever compromise. She tigers words
with frisky then hard-hitting paws,

reiterates her threat and slams
the door off beam, then re-enters to stage
recriminations thrown out of the past
like lava boiling in her throat,

her hands dropped confrontationally to hips,
hair stormed over one shoulder, while he shuts
the knowledge of her out, obdurately
resists the face-up facts, sneers at her *bitch* –

and won't modulate power control,
but turns towards his mafiaed entourage
looking for consolation, shouts her down
and stamps the flowers he'd bought her underfoot.

Las Vegas Debacle

A rhinestoned gladiator's junk-fazed roll
segues across the ballroom's glacial blaze,
his Bill Belew jumpsuit's called Inca Gold,

he is the Hilton's magus drug-cocktailed
and underoctaved as he takes the floor
to Zarathustra as a mad prelude.

Putti and cherubs tackily drip gold
above an ersatz auditorium.
The Roman colonnade's sheened with Day-Glo.

Diner sophisticats flake lobster bisque,
then down forks for a racy 'Blue Suede Shoes',
a furry-balled bee-stung delivery

unknotted from a tightened diaphragm.
He seems recalled to his identity
in short attention spans, as though he surfed

a wobbly coma's momentary read-out,
before returning to the soapy lens
through which the audience are white pill-faced blanks

straitjacketed into black tux. He spoofs
a medley, then slow-burns 'Suspicious Minds',
staggering epic on a sonic pile.

The dexies keep on speeding through his heart,
he's Elvis now in triplicate mass-fat
the aura blazing round his sovereign part.

Elvis Listens to the Sex Pistols (1976)

Animalistic Reichstag,
the safetypinned gobster's
nihilistic neo-Nazi credo

chainsaws the airwaves,
a flagrant out-of-the-dustbin
swastikaed resurrection

a punked suzerainty
kicked in from the garage,
its two-chord abrasiveness

tattooing the listener
with barbed-wire incisions.
Belsen's a hotel

a holiday camp ethos,
the guests sprinkle ash
instead of fine sugar.

Elvis recoils
from undialogued noise,
its raw Zeitgeist viscera

proclaiming no future.
He's a showbiz venerator
ceremonially stagy

a spotlit virtuoso
disdainful of thrash.
He's the camp on a wedding cake

the rococo volute,
an icing-sugar frost flower
baroquely uncut.

He leaves Johnny Rotten
gagging on vitreol
and resets the station,

unaware that he's channelled
sonic history

a Dadaist melange

of punk glossolalia,
goes back to the music room
and sits at the piano.

The Last Tour

The Elephant King
slurred and aphasiac
triples his body
tears a strained hamstring.
Hotels are pharmacies,
his doctor a crow
undertakerishly beaky
with a hypodermic
and thumbprinted shadow
monitoring Demerol.
E is intransigently
self-medicated,
lachrymosally distraught –
never made a classic film
or a lasting record,
consumed by the fear
of eponymous oblivion,
who will remember
poppy ephemera
not even Linda
Priscilla or Ginger
or the Graceland epigoni
after his remains
blaze in purple thunder?
When he drops the microphone
it's irretrievable,
nothing co-ordinates
he swims in balance loss
spiralling vertigo.
He should be on an elephant
bushed with ostrich plumes,
the great immovable
on tonnage that rolls
out of Las Vegas
to percussive ceremonials
somewhere in the desert
under brilliant stars
the huge body lowered
by a circle of black cars.

Last Rites

Thunder was all the previous night, big noise.
Ionized decibels banged out of heat
like late Beethoven smashing ivories
to simulate an elephant stampede...

The ceiling's black and gold-green Naugahyde.
He's 250lb slack fat.
The black fake suede strips bleed along the walls:
his double-king-size bed's shaped like a jeep.

He's prayed, obliquely, anecdotally,
extraordinary life means extraordinary death.
Sometimes he hears a truck roar through his cells,
the headlights blazing into Tupelo

before the detonative crash.
His 20,000 drug hits in three years
have morphed his chemistry. His brainfade furs.
The monitor's silent dialectic

is news from nowhere. He's walked round the room,
massaged, but never comes up clear.
He's like an elephant laid out to die,
his daughter hopping on the mound,

summitted up above the world.
The crimson coverlet's stage-curtain red;
the sepia-toned picture of Gladys blurs
to vanishing. He casts around for speech

that's free-associated. It's the tour
keeps dragging as an undertow.
He'll never make it. He's spotlit inside,
found out, and wanted on a different road.

It's sleep to which he gravitates,
as though a swimmer struck out for a reef
in moonlight, pulled himself on shore
and found the dream was absolutely real.

Black Limo Blues

Suppose he reversed his ending,
insighted the funeral limo's ceremonially
dilatory crawl to Forest Hill Cemetery,
he in a cream-coloured suit
in a copper casket to match his mother's
the frost in his hair retouched by mascara,
blue suit and striped tie punctiliously formal,
as though dressed correctly for acceptance
in heaven, and the massive heat
stunning the catatonically lachrymose mourners
corteged for three miles, a girl in lavender
holding a guitar made from red roses,
others kneeling in breezy ghost,
scratching the sky-face with importunate prayer,
willing him back like feeding a rope
over a cliff edge to fish for the drowned.
And the day footaged into history –
The King is Dead rising like a bee-toned
mantra across continents,
heard even in unmediatized swamplands,
and carried by birds to jungle interiors.
Suppose he began at this end,
danced his way out of the mausoleum
discarding experience like reject shirts,
retrieved his knee-jerking, jackknifing stance,
his blue downpour of hair at Overton Park,
his hormonal torrent buzzing the Hayride,
returned to gauchely conceived beginnings,
then he would have realized love and death
meet in exacting magnification,
the way forward and back always the same,
lit by a paparazzi's flash,
impossible now, impossible then,
but beautiful the way an actress holds
twenty red roses to herself
the moment before the impending crash.

He's Gone Away

Mostly at night, a train's annotation
of the dark dialogues with loss,
the millisecond lag time feeding sound
                      into
looped memories. I know he's on the train,
a single, insomniac passenger
anecdoting stage-triumphs to a guard
who hasn't slept for thirty years.
The carriage windows are blacked out, the seats
are sumptuous purple velvet monogrammed
with hieroglyphics. Red sequined cushions
retrieved from Graceland panoply his head.
The train stops at no nocturnal station,
                      reduces speed
on passing through each shut-down terminal,
then clatters through a bearish tree-tunnel
of interlacing antlered oaks. A gold stag
stares at oncoming lights and bolts
into dense rainy spray. The passenger
keeps looking out for Memphis. Thirty years
of circumnavigating track
and still the place eludes his homecoming
or is name-changed, disinformational
or relocated on a virtual map.
They shunt a coffin off the rails
and later on another one. There's been a war
or excavation of a cemetery?
and someone in a bloodstained sheet
is waving by the line. The train retrieves
a rolling speed; Elvis's purple suit's
accordioned from being sedentary;
the rhythm's regularized, the same old thing
reinstating staccato rap.
I listen to it go like music cut,
and leave dead Elvis looking out through rain
for Memphis or familiar signs,
the darkness swimming back, and in my dream
I'm nightbound, roof-surfing that winning train.

Mortuary Blues

Baronially coffined
ceremonialized in the music room
Mama's dressed in blue chiffon
Max Factor fixed for her son's
ululating lamentation,
he lies on the glass lid
morbidly necrophilic
like a voyeur at a window
repeating an obsession
or a man breaking ice
to access the abyss.
He cradles her feet
as though reading meridians
toenails lacquered scarlet
they're his pedic fixation,
small as though raised in Chinese
bandages, manicured sooties
he lip-feeds repeatedly.
She's his psychic heartbeat,
he's a shamanic journeyer
gone with her
as she crosses over,
leaves Memphis for a starlit
mansion without address
wallpapered he imagines
with pictures of Elvis.
Dissociated, tranced,
he's zombified numb
crouched over the casket,
then dressed for the funeral
in understated chocolate
is disconsolately lachrymose
lifted by harmonies
the Blackwood Brothers
singing 'Precious Memories'
elusively all
that's left him in Forest Hill Cemetery,
down flat on his knees
screaming valedictory
rites as they hem earth over the coffin.

Birthday in Heaven

He's ectoplasmic posthumous
a hoodooed Francis Bacon
slap at a voodoo hex
concealed in the bluey features,
a birthday out of time
cake-remastered by Gladys,
every star in the sky
torching a celebration.
Elvis wearing a suit
of pink roses in his mansion,
checks his archival website
for interplanetary e-mail,
knows from romantic transmissions
he's still hero-revered on earth,
although his contact's selective
and getting through's infrequent.
Today, he'll close-encounter
a contactee called Deborah,
infiltrate her mind-set
until pick-up registers,
snow into her subtle
easily accessed visual,
a bluish glow as a halo
helping his image earth.
He's exultantly postfamous,
but misses his car-stable
and the kitsch-grove at Graceland
rippling with banana puddings.
Elvis's telepresent date
is dyeing her hair when he calls,
hennaering her roots orange
with mud-paste fingers:
he virtualizes full face
as a walk-in intruder,
tells her her haircolour's great
only grow it to the shoulder,
communicates through psi-love
a deepening like a colour
that goes on increasing the way
ivy bleeds its hearts round a gate.

The New

Disinherits itself
from every precinct
even Elvis seems
too singularly decade-
conscious, image-passé
superseded, like faces
seen as print out in the street
and burnt off in the instant,
never re-encountered
or polarized again.
Nothing's retrievably
reinstantiated,
no isotropic thought
backlit by reflection,
no entrée on the stairs
in a backless red gown,
no wind-morphed cumulus
sculpted from vapour
bottoming over
a corporate high-rise.
Snails attempt to drug
time into slow motion
their glitter-alphabet
a graffito's Sanskrit
puzzled from trance
in viscous filigree.
Everything's post-dated
because it's of the moment,
the mauve shoe, the blue shoe,
the hemline's tidemark.
Elvis is on time-hold
like spike-haired Johnny Rotten
or a model sashaying
an exit from the catwalk,
the image is upgraded,
the new's in the raindrop
lemony, alive
in its sparkling hit
to the testy hand extended
as a bounce-off target.

ELVITES: THE CULT

Daughters of the Precious Blood

They came together in sorority
through cultic interests, fanzines, underworlds,
converted a Victorian house, one drove
a revamped hearse, bodywork airbrushed pink,

proclaiming Elvis as E faith,
the church of rhinestoned mystery;
and if Vanessa pricked a drop of blood
into a sugar cube, the King would show,
in little ways, a healing touch,
an ostentatious ring found in a shoe,

a white wall turned temporarily blue.
Six of them housed together, ate black food,
dressed with iconic style, and kept apart,
resisting contact. Rumours mobbed the street,
a private chapel, the one with pink hair
seen buying diamonds by the fist,
Internet sightings, Elvis seen
in dark glasses at a departure gate,

but never making it on to the flight.
One day the six joined hands out in the street,
a sunflower grew up on the spot
as token of the mystery,
E's mournful eye inside the perianth.

They kept the house a year, clean moved one night,
but left behind a voice, and it would sing
to spook the curious, those moody blue

big ballads immortalized by the King.

E Sightings

A stillness in the noon, a white-out blank,
an interference in earth's frequencies,
the radio music leaked from Mars
for nanoseconds, then the right
restored, the poppy's radar dish
turned to a foggy sun again,

the black Lincoln refiring on the road,
the plane regaining altitude.
A spookish body-double's on the prowl,
a lookalike, satin-shirted vampire,

a freak with neurons, but no heart
frog-kicking in the diaphragm.
He never stays, the glimpse is flashed
or VRd into consciousness,
but once he came on in a club,
sang 'Burning Love', let the shock waves subside

and on the instant dematerialized.
Once in an airport lounge he signed
his name invisibly, panicked,
and two blue sequins dropped out of his eyes,

two teardrop-shaped scintillations.
He's kept here by impacted psychic charge,
a nowhere figure in-betweened
and bottoming, a revenant

reminded of his fame
in blinding snatches, never freed
of bites at temporality,
and back tonight, tucked in a black Lincoln,
remembers too much, as the car
journeys across a foreign continent
as though its aimed to catch a falling star.

Elvis and the UFO Conspiracy

A speed-up recall dart fired in his neck,
he reads an intraspecies graffiti,
signals downloaded from a biosphere,
transcription factors written in his cells
and digitally impulsed on the screen...

He scans the near asteroid-belt
for mutant lookalikes. They brought him here,
an abductee inside a ship
bluely lit up by terminals,

and placed an implant in his brain,
to track his neural drive. He looks at Mars,
its oxidized iron-ferric red soils
under construction; a new launching site

is being worked, the footage spots
with mad-whirl of a solar storm,
planetary glitter, sonic dust.
They've tagged him, and will monitor

neuronal input of a king.
He's fazed, and tugs the sequined gown
they've thrown around him, blue sequins
splashy with decorative gold stars.
He thinks he's dreaming, but the needle jabs

him into awareness it's real,
the blood sample, DNA test,
the aliens dressed in holographic suits
attendant on him.
                            He flips out

and wakes alone beside the road.
He's miles from nowhere; raffish fields
are hay-bleached blond. He hears a plane,

and runs towards it, arms raised to the sky.

Lonely Street

The mood is mostly blue to indigo
inside a heart-shaped bar, and three or four
habitués sit facing a mirror
on which a red-lipsticked calligraphy
has upper-cased the words Heartbreak Hotel,

and lower, Desolation Avenue.
The men are Elvis lookalikes,
arrogating a desultory, mean,
extended teenage defiance,

collars turned up, working perversity
into an image of untouchable
hauteur, a sex not love response
should someone's eyes flirtatiously
catch theirs across the smoky bar.

The girls are archetypal dolls,
mascaraed, mouths shaped into hearts,
leggily rearranging hems,

equally inaccessible.
Strangers arrive, and moodily
select their corner of the room;
a red jacket splashed in a cobalt chair,
a pair of dark glasses hiding a face,

a fifties jukebox with its Presley stash
inviting all to feed blue memories.
The legend runs, Elvis returns each year,
anonymously rhinestoned in the bar,

sits hunched over, without saying a word,
assimilates his old records, goes out,

and leaves a trail of diamonds to his car.

Desolation Avenue

The wind is always back of January,
an open Steinway dominates the street
inviting an impromptu hand
to jam a bluesy elegy.
The King is searching for Liberace,

he sights a screen goddess, another one,
ankle-length furs, recherché paste,
scouting for taxis. There's a desert jeep

parked by the boarded liquor store,
its only eye a mounted gun.
He wants extemporaneous song,
tuber roots in atavistic gospel,

a celebration to climb on his breath.
The avenue's telescoped linearity
goes on for ever. There's no break

or parallel as an option
to its monotonous trajectory.
The store windows are empty black mirrors,
Las Vegas as a flawed diamond,
the movie posters obsolete,

Veronica Lake, Jayne Mansfield,
a macho, masochistic, cool James Dean.
The King's overconspicuous,
his body's full of liquid nitrogen,

but still his heart pumps like a fish,
a deoxygenating red snapper.
He needs to get back to real time
or freeze into an exhibit –

a rock'n'roll
jewelled monolith preserved by ice.

Michael Jackson

He wants to be La Toya. It's her face
he copies by the line, a geometry
that eliminates gender, points the way
to a reconstructed species. He's high
on dance, the generated pheromones

leave him ecstatic. It's a solitary
exploration of inner light, the beat
of an automated android consumed
by mirror images – he's reflected
everywhere in the mansion, and his feet

won't walk, they look for rhythm, instate speed.
Reclusive, air-sealed by security,
a legend to himself out in LA,
surrounded by Pharaonic monuments,
an emperor's exotic menagerie,

Hollywood mannequins, he's grown into
the ultimate parody of a star,
military jackets splashed with braid, his eyes
shielded by dark glasses, a permanent
regression back to youth – how can he age

inside the dream that he's alive? He sits
beside a panther. He's always on stage.
The world outside is a receding point,
an abstract notion, and the drum machine
is on, computing faultless dance-floor hits.

Jackson/Presley Legacy

In a hyperbaric tent
he's post-biologized.
Prosthetic anatomy
a VR escapee.

Lipstick, foundation,
grape-bunched dreadlocks.
His genes are the I Ching
predicting no gender.

A telepresent
marriage to Lisa Marie.
The Di doll on display
wears a tiara.

A sip at the Presleys
through teleportation,
she sends him red balloons
and he returns black ones.

In the Egyptian bathroom
at Dean Gardens
the new King mascaras
on a Ramses throne.

He's the ersatz Elvis
in military scarlet,
graphite earpieces
transmitting a dance groove.

A glitz table is set
for a teddybear's picnic,
the Hamleys carriers
stuffed with toy walk-ins.

She's Elvis-present
in his pop vampirism
unreal as fame
to his solitary dynasty.

Elvis Crowned by Martians

18-wheel big rigs silver on the site.
Elvis's post-bio sauna's moussy
with dermal collagenic plant protein

a Glico-Lift Full Face Patch impregnates
AHA into desiccated pores.
The grey ones implant humanoidish genes,

bump up his enzymes for galactic haul.
The Karin Herzog Vit-A-Kombi cream
oxygenates blue billiards pockets

cavy like swimming pools beneath the eyes.
He's psyched to Martianize, download his sperm
for Elvite banks. He likes the bronze zoot suit.

They have his earthworks stored on memory.
Red discs not gold emblazon a cabin.
The drips will readjust brain chemistry.

The ceremony's done with a syringe;
E's injected with deathlessness.
The star-shot heavens blaze into his veins.

He's crowned with red stones. Back on virtual Mars,
reconnaissance across a pyramid
shows greys aware of the terrestrial King.

They watch it back home on miniplexed screens,
intergalactic history live from Earth,
planetary dust storms blowing in between.

Elvisians From Other Planets

Website evangelists –
this one surfs for freaky, drop-in
humanoids. Pompadour faithful
he artefacts jam donuts on a plate
like Martian deposit.

Alien Elvisians
communicate through shared favourites,
netting the solar system
for contact. Long live the King's
their password to a Las Vegas theatre,

a database auditorium.
This hacker's website's invaded
by Jupiterian clone-doners,
DNA replicators,
coding the King's double helices on screen.

He's seasonal affective,
VR solitary in Elvite vigil.
He waits for cross-pollinated sonics
a Plutonian remix
of 'Love Me Tender'.

He fortunes by his terminal
a talismanic memento,
a carved totemic hamburger
that wards off coronary evils
induced by hectares of fried food.

Elvis is artery scrubbed
with the out-theres, telemedically
repaired, miked to the galaxy.
His devotional hacker
fries food in saturated butter.

THE UNPUBLISHED SONGBOOK

Hootchy Kootchy (1959)

I was born with good luck
on a mean hard street
got chased out of shadows
by a rock'n'roll beat
Hootchy Kootchy, hootchy kootchy
makes me smoochy
smoochy all night long

My baby she worked
bought me a guitar
got some high-heel boots
now I'm a rock'n'roll star
Hootchy Kootchy, hootchy kootchy
makes me smoochy
smoochy all night long

My woman she left me
for a man in a bar
they sped out of town
in a big black car
Hootchy Kootchy, hootchy kootchy
makes me smoochy
smoochy all night long

I was playin' a club
when my baby walked in
she had tears in her eyes
and a look of sin
Hootchy Kootchy, hootchy kootchy
makes me smoochy
smoochy all night long

Took my baby outside
said she loved me true
she was all broke up
brokenhearted and blue
Hootchy Kootchy, hootchy kootchy
makes me smoochy
smoochy all night long

The next day I gave
my woman a ring
got up on the stage
and I started to sing
Hootchy Kootchy, hootchy kootchy
makes me smoochy
smoochy all night long

Black and White (1957)

A smalltown boy, he made it big
came on as a star
in the local bar
He wasn't black or white tonight
alright, he wasn't black or white
in a barroom fight alright

His baby swore to shoot him dead
he was up on the stage
like a lion in a cage
He wasn't black or white tonight
alright, he wasn't black or white
in a barroom fight alright

She found him with another girl
they were smoochin' slow
when the lights were low
He wasn't black or white tonight
alright, it wasn't black or white
in a barroom fight alright

She took her time and bought a gun
kept it right by her bed
to shoot him dead
It wasn't black or white tonight
alright, he wasn't black or white
in a barroom fight alright

In a smoky joint she raised the gun
he was into a song
three minutes' long
He wasn't black or white tonight
alright, it wasn't black or white
in a barroom fight alright

A smalltown boy, he died that night
came on as a star
in the local bar
He wasn't black or white tonight
alright, it wasn't black or white
in a barroom fight alright

Knee Jerk (1951)

Saw the glory comin'
did the knee jerk knee jerk
down on my knees

Shook my hips like a snake
did the knee jerk knee jerk
down on my knees

Saw this big cat prowlin'
did the scratch jerk scratch jerk
down on my knees

Heard a big bike roarin'
did the speed jerk knee jerk
down on my knees

Went out on the road
did the knee jerk teen jerk
down on my knees

Saw the glory comin'
did the scratch jerk teen jerk knee
jerk down on my knees

Danced the whole night long
did the knee jerk knee jerk
down on my knees

Saw this big cat prowlin'
did the miaow jerk miaow jerk
scratchin' my knees

Looked up at the heavens
did the knee jerk knee jerk
prayin' on my knees

Saw the glory comin'
did the knee jerk knee jerk
down on my knees

Pink Cadillac

I'ze drivin' down the highway
in a pink Cadillac
got chrome on the bonnet
black suede in the back
saw this blonde by the roadside
she's swinging her hips
got the wind in her hair
and bee-stung lips

Gonna dance on the bonnet
'til she turns her head
she's wearin' blue jeans
and her lips are red
Gonna dance on the bonnet
in my high-heel boots

Pulled the car to a halt
my pink Cadillac
she was clicking her heels
but she didn't look back
I stood on the roof
with my legs spread wide
gonna burn up the road
take her for a ride

Gonna dance on the bonnet
'til she turns her head
she's wearin' blue jeans
and her lips are red
Gonna dance on the bonnet
in my high-heel boots

Well she turned around
but she wouldn't stay
looked at her blonde hair
it was blown away
Got back in my Cadillac
chrome shone like the sun
we burned down the highway
'til the day was done

Gonna keep on drivin'
 til I find that girl
Gonna keep on drivin'
to the end of the world
[Gonna keep on searchin'
for that blonde-haired girl]

Diggin' My Heart (1958)

Well the pink moon shone
on the bad side of town
I bin diggin' my heart
goin' down and down
what I find inside
ain't nothin' like gold
my baby she's gone
left me in the cold

I'm goin' down and down
goin' down and down
got a one-way ticket
to the bad side of town

Well I bought this lot
on Dead End Street
I bin diggin' my heart
'til I'm really beat
couldn't buy no bricks
couldn't raise a roof
and the rain came down
on the bitter truth

I'm goin' down and down
goin' down and down
got a one-way ticket
to the bad side of town

Well I told my Mamma
had to catch the train
I bin diggin' my heart
and feelin' the pain
I gone down to my roots
and my heart is bare
I bin lookin' for my baby
but she ain't there

I'm goin' down and down
goin' down and down
got a one-way ticket
to the bad side of town

Well I'm down the line
and I can't turn round
I bin diggin' my heart
in the lost and found
couldn't buy no bricks
couldn't raise a roof
and the rain came down
on the bitter truth

I'm goin' down and down
goin' down and down
got a one-way ticket
to the bad side of town

Southern Blues (1957)

Baby, I gotta woman
she wears high-heel shoes
she walks like a stripper
and she give(s) me the blues
Baby, I gotta woman
but I'm gonna lose

I drive a pink Cadillac
Baby, am I smart
I got holes in my feelings
and a love-bruised heart
Baby, I gotta woman
dunno where to start

Baby, I'm shook up
and my house is on fire
she walks like a stripper
and I melt with desire
Baby, I gotta woman
and she ain't for hire

I'm an unschooled boy
but I aim for the stars
Baby, I gotta woman
and a string of big cars
I drive a pink Cadillac
play pool in the bars

Baby, I gotta woman
she wears high-heel shoes
she eats my heart on a fork
and she give(s) me the blues
Baby, I gotta woman
but I'm gonna lose

Hurtin' Boy (1956)

She leaves me lonely all the day
Mamma I'm her hurtin' boy
she uses up my railroad pay
Mamma I'm her broken toy
she uses up my railroad pay

She leaves me crying in the rain
Mamma I'm so broken down
she never eases up the pain
Mamma I'm all over town
she never eases up the pain

She leaves me calling on the Lord
Mamma I'm a wasted youth
she's thrown away my whisky hoard
Mamma it's the bitter truth
she's thrown away my whisky hoard

She's dressed up shocking for her date
Mamma he is my best friend
with me she's always cruel and late
Mamma how I wish an end
with me she's always cruel and late

She's killing me coz she's untrue
Mamma get your boy a gun
she makes me broken-hearted blue
Mamma help your only son
she makes me broken-hearted blue

She leaves me lonely all the day
Mamma I'm her hurtin' boy
her black clothes are my judgement day
Mamma I'm her broken toy
her black clothes are my judgement day

ELVIS'S LEGACY

Elvis's Legacy

From the body dispersal. It's a gold foundation
                              to a rock'n'roll
institution, a Presley academy's
universal studio, Elvis's larynx and hyoid
                              bone
built into copyist spontaneity;
it's a god-spot he occupies on the airwaves,
                              a sonic apotheosis
for blue velvet-throated crooners,
a seamless legacy where black and white R & B
                              appealers
to healing-archetypes unite.
He's cited in unconscious dialogue like a
                              blue brooch
pinned to the heart. He's always undiminished
like it's on stage 1956, his flamingo-pink
                              jacket
flipping in time like a cocktail shaker
diffusing a Campari-based slow-
                              burner,
an evening sky turned muddled raspberry
                              over mountains.
He's the reconstituted dionysian
in ankle-length leopardskin digitalized
                              on recall
like a head thrown over a shoulder captures
                              dark looks
in shocking pink St Laurent in a wet
                              street
late afternoon. He's the infrastructural pivot
to tearjerker pop, the irrepressible baritone
built on as heritage; listen to them in the dark
                              on Jazz FM
or in the cobalt standout heroic timbre of
                              Scott Walker
pitching a ballad to indigo tone.
He's the central pillar to a vocal scaffolding,
roofing the world with inconsequential hits,
                              sassy, transient,
but implanted in the blue collective,

a sound vocabulary increasing each decade.
Elvis is somatic rhythm, a revamped body
                              danced on
when lilacs wave their heady tusks, or a full
                              claret rose
distributes skirts over a garden urn.
His vocal fingerprint retros time to timeless
                              summer days
of prototypical pop. Collar the decades
and turn them around in their fifties, sixties jackets,
they're all wearing Elvis sport coats
and bright-red shoes. He's burnt his face for ever
                              on iconic
legend, the tragic, the glamorized, the suicided
                              out,
the monumental on a bolt of gold silk
poured from the sun, the extravagantly risqué
eating caviar off toes in the deep leather
                              interior
of a stretch limousine. He's pink satin louche
to androgynous neophytes, any sort of sex
he has them kneeling. In the Church of Sequined
                              Hearts
or the First Presleyterian Church of Elvis the Divine,
they're celebrating the *puer*, the youth who lives
                              for ever
as an oak tree throws its shadow
year after year. He's the futuristic blueprint
for ostentatious Vegas cabaret
the diamonds and emeralds bigger than a
                              mountain range
on manicured fingers.
He'll be present at the end of time, the final
dénouement, the breaking of the champagne glass
on an eagle's summit, the cortege of funeral
                              cars
tracking through the valley, carrying a black suit
and a gold microphone, and a thousand red
                              roses
for a singer's grave. He's the orphic resurrection
if you hear the tune, the melodic poppy
                              number

stretched across the sky, the first and the last
chosen pop-romantic out on the road
of eternal return. Look up, and he might be
                                there
as a sign in the stars, an adventitious arrival
elected as messiah in a gold Cadillac
kicking up a dust trail right across the world.
He'll lean out of a window and lower dark
                                shades
and wave to someone running in pursuit of the
                                car,
a girl with stilettos bunched in her hands
like two small animals, and tracking hard,
sure that it's him, while the wasteland applauds,
and an oak tree curtsies level with the road,
swings back violently and throws up its arms.

DANCING IN
THE STREET

Juicy Lucy Cannibalizes Elvis

A rumoured body-snatch
for necrophagous predators
the Dead King exhumed

compounded into burgers
liver, kidney, cerebellum
every bit matters

sold in labelled boxes
from the depot mincer
Lucy moon-mouths tissue

from a sacrosanct thigh
her throat's a hypogeum
for majesterial gristle

her gut's the inner sanctum
for the King's resurrection
she takes him in flakily

savouring each particle's
ketchuped veneer
masticates the cocktail

prays as it goes down
Lucy's Sister Tender
to the cannibal church

Elvis in the freezer
in limited number burgers
is necromantic sustenance

to her weirdo libido
thinking she'll rebirth
her quiffy hero

Resurrectional Cryonics

The nano-revamped E-brain's
repaired in liquid nitrogen
a deep-freeze fishy organ

coded from bio-remains
of informational DNA
it's made Elvis-responsive

reanimated software
molecularly cloned
a site for restoration

rather like the Pharaohs
glyphed their vibrant info
into funeral jewels

jades and jet and turquoise
brimming with their neurons
a compact chemistry

morgued for retrieval
E's the mega-avatar
charisma-tested

the most wanted revival
of transtime resurrectees
studied for his U-turns

between brain hemispheres
they're doing it at Alcor
post-rigor-mortis shuffle

throwing switches in his mind
so he'll do a Pentecostal
in the virtual lab.

Dancing in the Street

His century disappears as dead footage,
fragmented masters in the can,
a junked and displaced memorabilia

disassembled by history,
the virtualized still doing it
computer concerts on a giant screen.

The all-shook-up divinity's
performing redubbed hits.
He's real-time absent: a body-bagged kit.

Sundays resemble a Swiss chocolate bar,
the taste of leisure sweet, the tang
of undertow a bitter dark,

a day for dancing in the street
to lift an urban polity
to dance-points in the toxic haze.

They're matching it in a car park
the new groove on an Elvis beat:
the sunlight reads its face in a mirror

and keeps on polishing
a photon-zoomed insignia
across a dark green Jaguar.

Two kids have got new Elvis right
amongst pollutants, scratchcard drift
and buzz-dance in the wasted violet light.